Happy F  ning Centre

A play

John Godber

Smuel London
New York

ISBN 0 573 01782 4

Please see page iv for further copyright information.

HAPPY FAMILIES

Commissioned by British Telecom for the Little Theatre Guild of Great Britain, the play was subsequently rewritten and performed professionally at the West Yorkshire Playhouse in February 1992, with the following cast of characters:

John	Nick Lane
Dot	Judith Barker
Vic	Andrew Livingstone
Liz	Marcia Warren
Jack	Wilfred Grove
Aunty Doris	Jane Clifford
Aunty Edna	Maggie Lane
Rebecca	Henrietta Voigts
Lyn Sutton	Henrietta Voigts

Directed by John Godber
Designed by Rob Jones

First BT Biennial 1991

Happy Families received forty-nine simultaneous premières by members of the Little Theatre Guild of Great Britain in October 1991.

CHARACTERS

John; ages from nine to twenty-five
Dot, John's mother; ages from forty to fifty-four
Vic, John's father; ages from forty to fifty-four
Liz, John's grandmother; ages from sixty to seventy-four
Jack, John's grandfather; ages from sixty to seventy-four
Doris, John's mucky aunty; ages from thirty to forty-four
Edna, John's posh aunty; ages from forty to fifty-four
Rebecca, John's genius cousin; ages from eleven to
    twenty-five
Lyn Sutton, aged seven

The action takes place in a house in West Yorkshire

ACT I   The years 1967–1973
ACT II   The years 1975–1978

SETTING

The setting is a house with large spaces for doors, no actual doors. A sofa c, a table, three chairs and an easy chair. All the furniture is treated in the same colour tone. The house is a "memory house."

Other plays by John Godber published by Samuel French Ltd

Salt Of The Earth
Teechers
Up 'N' Under

ACT I

A Living-Room

The room is carpeted and painted cream, its features blurred slightly, as if seen in memory; it is not realistic, but quite definitely a theatrical set. There is an exit UL. C *is a sofa; other furniture is set out in appropriate positions*

As the play begins, music from the late nineteen sixties is playing. The cast enter and take up positions around the stage

John sits on the sofa; he is wearing a suit for his university graduation. Dot begins to clean the floor with a vacuum cleaner (which has no lead); she is dressed in clothes from the nineteen sixties

The music fades

Vic enters

Vic She's at it again.
Dot What?
Vic Look at you.
Dot I want it to be nice for your Edna coming. (*She stops cleaning the floor and begins to polish the furniture*)
John (*to the audience*) My mother was cleaning, as usual, and my dad stood watching her in disbelief. She'd already hoovered that part of the carpet a hundred times.
Vic Do you have to go crackers every day?
John (*to the audience*) She did, it was a disease.
Vic I mean you're nearly through to the floorboards.
John (*to the audience*) But my dad had learnt to live with her; my mother would always tell him:
Dot You can't plan housework. An house has a life of its own. I don't work shifts, Vic, I'm on call all the time. Now go and put the kettle on ...
Vic It won't fit me.
John (*to the audience*) My dad's jokes were only funny once, but he told them a thousand times.
Vic Dot, this Indian right, walks into a trading post, "Oh, my head." Trading post, wood, get it, a wooden post?

Jack enters slowly, carrying a pair of garden clippers. He is a strong, dour character

Jack These garden clippers need sharpening, Vic.
Vic Right-oh, Pa.

Vic exits with the clippers

John (*to the audience*) And then there was my grandad, who was a real myth. He was a maniac and would fight any man, anywhere.

Liz enters the scene. She has a duster in her hand

Liz Have you finished them hedges?
Jack Ar.
Liz Have you made a good job?
Jack Ar.
Liz Go and cut the lawns.
Jack Ar.

   Jack silently exits

Liz is left, flicking her duster

John (*to the audience*) My grandmother was a bundle of love and affection. She had bone cancer in later life but she never told anyone.
Liz I think I'll have a cuppa tea, Doris.

   Liz exits

   Doris enters, knitting

Doris It's brewing, Mam, I'm just seeing to it.
John (*to the audience*) This is my Aunty Doris, she's my mucky aunty.
Doris I'm knitting our John another tank top, nip.
Dot (*off*) Lovely.

   Doris exits

   Edna enters, sipping her tea

John (*to the audience*) My Aunty Doris knitted constantly, but she had a problem with sizes.
Edna This is lovely. It really is lovely tea, Dorothy. Is it Rington's?
John (*to the audience*) My posh Aunty Edna lived in Gloucester. She'd left Yorkshire and married a man from Cambridge. She worked with cancer patients all her life and was a cut above the rest.
Edna It's a long drive but we like to make the effort to come "home".

   Rebecca, aged eleven, enters. She carries a clarinet

Rebecca I like going to see Aunty Dot and Uncle Vic, they're so sweet.
Edna Go on, Rebecca, play something.
John (*to the audience*) Rebecca was my cousin. She was supposed to be a child genius.

   Edna and Rebecca exit, Rebecca playing "You Make Me Feel So Young" appallingly as she goes

Dot begins to hum the tune

John (*to the audience*) It was nineteen-sixty-seven. And in nineteen-sixty-seven I was waiting for a letter that would shape my life forever.

John exits

Dot sings a verse of "You Make Me Feel So Young"

   Vic enters. He is carrying a letter and is very excited

Vic It's here. It's here.

Dot Settle down, you'll have a bloody stroke. (*She stops cleaning*)

Vic It's here, it's come. I've just seen t' postwoman.

Dot Well, open it.

Vic I'm shaking.

Dot Give it to me.

Vic No, I want to read it. I've been waiting for this to come. Where is he? Is he in t' garden?

Dot He's kicking that ball about.

Vic Shout him in.

Dot Look at you, you're like a big kid, now stop getting over-excited. (*She shouts*) John? John, what are you doing, where are you?

John, dressed in shorts and a very large tank top, enters

Vic Your letter's come, kid. Results from school.

Dot Well, open it, we haven't got all day.

John (*to the audience*) I'm eleven and I'm bloody nervous.

Vic (*opening the letter*) Here we are ... (*He reads*) "Dear Mr and ..." Yeah, blah blah. Here we are ... "to inform you that John has been successful in achieving a place at ..." (*His voice changes; he sounds desperately disappointed*) "Clifton Secondary Modern School. Term commences September the thirteenth, nineteen-sixty-seven."

There is a silence

Dot Right.

Vic Oh, well ...

Another silence

Dot (*with a massive sigh*) Oh, dear ...

Another silence

Vic Shall we get cleaned up?

Dot We'd better. Oh, John.

John (*to Dot*) What does it mean, Mam?

Dot It means you're not going to grammar school. Come here, what are we going to make of you, eh?

Vic It means you've failed, kid. Failed your eleven-plus.

John I can't even remember taking it.

Vic Typical of our John, he can't even remember taking it, he probably didn't take it. I bet he was playing bloody football that day.

Dot (*slowly*) I could belt him.

Vic Don't start it ...

Dot I could ...

Vic Leave him alone.

Dot I could belt you. I could, Vic, he's got me all on edge.

Vic Do you think I couldn't?

Dot Well, belt him then.

Vic You belt him.

Dot You, my lad, you, you ...

John What?

Dot You little thing ...

Vic Leave him.

Dot A failure.

Vic I said leave him.

Dot Failed his eleven-plus, I just can't believe it.

Vic I knew.

Dot A failure.

Vic He's not a failure.

Dot Well, what is he then?

Vic He's my lad.

Dot He's my lad too.

Vic I thought you were supposed to love him?

Dot I do.

Vic Well, shut up then.

John (*to the audience*) They were right and I knew it. I was a failure. Thrown out at eleven. I think it made it worse when my family found out how many had passed.

Vic (*loudly*) Two.

Dot Don't go on.

Vic Two.

Dot If you say two again I'll scream.

Vic Two. Two kids fail in a class of thirty-two and our John is one of them?

John (*to the audience*) It was a good year.

Vic And he's supposed to be intelligent. You said making him go to bed early would make him intelligent.

Dot That's what my mother did with me.

Vic And look at you.

Dot I went to bed early every night.

Vic So what?

Dot Me and our Doris were always in bed by seven.

Vic What's that got to do with the price of eggs?

Dot And we got up early, not like you.

Vic I get up before you.

Dot Right, my lad, you will go to bed early for the rest of your life.

Vic Too late now, isn't it?

Dot He can go to bed early tonight, anyway.

There is a pause

Vic How come Denis Smeaton passed and he didn't, how come? His dad's a postman! How come Tony Baines passed? Lyn Sutton next door passed. Keith Eastmoor is going to be a dentist. Andrew West is going to be a vet. Mrs Thompson told me that her son is going to walk on the moon.

Dot Don't be ridiculous.
Vic How come they passed and he didn't?
Dot He probably sat the wrong exam, knowing our John.

Vic and Dot exit in silence

John (*to the audience*) I knew I was a no-hoper. Two years earlier I'd been playing "Doctors and Nurses" next door with Lyn Sutton.

Lyn Sutton enters. She is seven years old, a coy girl with a bow in her hair, short socks and a dress

Lyn I've got a pain, Doctor.
John (*to the audience*) I loved this game.
Lyn I've got this pain. I've got an awful pain in my body.
John (*to Lyn*) Where is it?
Lyn On my body, Doctor.
John Where, Nurse?
Lyn Somewhere.
John Is it here? (*He touches the top of her chest, very slowly and shyly*)
Lyn No.
John Is it here? (*He moves his hand slowly down her chest*)
Lyn No, Doctor. It's not there. And it hurts me when I breathe.
John Does it?
Lyn Yes, it does.
John (*moving his hand to lightly touch her breast*) Is it here?
Lyn Yes. That's it, Doctor. That's much better.
John Well, you had better take two tablets a day, Nurse, and if the pain comes back you had better come and see me again. Thank you. Next please.
Lyn Now you.
John What?
Lyn Now you. Show me.
John I haven't got any pains. Besides, I'm the doctor.
Lyn Show me.
John What?
Lyn You know.
John I don't.
Lyn Your whatsit?
John No.
Lyn I've shown you mine.
John Your what?
Lyn Thing.
John Oh, yeah ... urghhh.
Lyn Come on ... I'll be the doctor, and you come and have to show me.
John Oh, all right. (*John begins to take off his trousers, revealing British Home Stores underwear. He prepares to show his manhood to Lyn but ...*)

Dot enters, coming only a little way onstage

Dot John! John!

John (*grabbing at his trousers, panic-stricken*) Oh no.
Dot John, are you there? Tea's ready.
John Yeah ...
Dot Your Aunty Edna's come to see us.
John Oh crikey, oh no ...

Dot exits

The introduction to Alma Cogan's "Hernando's Hideaway" begins to play

John exits, attempting to put on his trousers

Lyn exits in the opposite direction

The Lights fade and then come up on Edna, Dot, Vic and Doris having tea

Dot Does anybody want any spring onion? Anybody? Would you like some beetroot, Edna?
Edna No thank you. I'm quite happy with this cup of tea, Dorothy, thanks. Is it Rington's?
Dot No, it's Typhoo. I got it from Denis Richards, he's got a little shop on the corner. His mother's in a wheelchair. They're really nice people. Wouldn't say boo to a goose.
Edna Oh, I see.
Dot Would you like an Eccles cake?
Edna No thanks.
Dot They're nice.
Edna No, really.
Dot Are you sure?
Edna Positive. I've already had far too many.
Dot You've only had one.

Edna does not answer, just sips her tea

Doris Does she want a tart? Give her a tart, our Dorothy, give her a tart. I've brought 'em; give her a tart. They're lovely.

John enters, his trousers back to front. He stands looking shyly at his family

Edna No, honestly, I couldn't. Honestly.
Dot (*to John*) Say hello to your Aunty Edna, don't just stand there like a drip.
John (*whispering*) Hello.
Vic He's shy, Edna. Say hello proper.
John (*in the same voice*) Hello.
Edna Hello, John, nice to see you. How are you?

John does not respond

Dot He's very shy.
Edna Are you. Are you shy?

John nods

Doris He's lovely, aren't you? I could eat him. He's a bit shy, Edna, but he'll grow out of it when he gets a bit older. He's been playing next door, haven't you? Been playing with the little girl next door. It's his girlfriend, isn't it?

John No.

Doris He knows it is.

Edna Rebecca sends her apologies, John, she wanted to come but her school have gone to Germany. They've gone to Germany for ten days. I think they're going to try and go ski-ing while they're out there.

Vic That sounds good, kid, eh?

Edna She's doing very well at the moment, Vic.

Vic Is she?

Edna She's doing *very well* at the moment.

Vic That's good to hear, isn't it, Dot?

Dot Doing well is she?

Edna She's doing very well. At the moment. We're not quite sure how it's going to go, but fingers crossed. This is really nice tea.

Dot It's Typhoo. It's not Rington's.

Edna is transfixed by John having his trousers on back to front

Edna John. I was just wondering if you knew that you have your trousers on the wrong way around. Did you know? They're on back to front? Did you know?

All the family have now become interested. John fidgets and tries to look innocent

John No.

Edna Well they are, unless they're rather special trousers? Are they?

John No.

Edna Oh.

Doris Oh, yeah they are ... It took me a minute to realize. He's probably made a mistake.

Vic Did you know that, John?

John Yeah. My gran bought them for me. They're new, they've got pockets in the back.

Dot Turn around.

John No.

Dot Turn around.

John Mam ... ?

Doris Are they new? They're lovely, I think.

Dot Turn around.

John reluctantly turns round; we see that the fly and zip of his trousers are at the back.

Doris That's good, they've got a zip at the back. They're lovely.

Dot (*sinister*) What have you been doing?

John Eh.

Dot Turn back around.

John turns back to face his mother

Doris I like the colour.
Dot What have you been doing?
John Nothing.
Dot You have.
John I haven't.
Dot What have you been playing at in there?
John Nothing.
Dot Don't lie. If you lie I'll hit you. If you tell me the truth I'll let you off.
John I haven't been doing nothing, Mam.
Vic (*whispering to Dot*) Leave him. Do you want some more tea, Edna?
Edna I'm fine.
Dot What's been going on?
John (*steeling himself to tell the story; he acts it out rather badly*) Well, it must have been a mistake, and when I pulled my trousers up, my body must have spun around and then it got stuck and I was facing the wrong way, and that must be what happened because my trousers are facing the wrong way, and my body was stuck and I got my head back the right way, and couldn't walk proper so I asked Lyn to pull my body back and I haven't taken my trousers off Mam, honest, she told me to and I didn't do it, she did it first anyway, because I was the doctor and I love you, Mam. And she made me do it.

There is a silence

Dot Go to bed.
John Yes, Mam.
Doris Oh, leave him.
Dot Go to bed.
John Aunty Doris?
Doris Oh, Dot, leave him, he's told you the truth. He wants to stay up.
Dot Bed.
John Yes, Mam.
Edna Aren't you going to say goodbye before you go?
John (*curtly*) Goodbye. (*He turns to go*)
Vic Hey, come back here and say goodbye properly to your Aunty Edna; let her see you've got some manners.
John Dad?
Vic What?
John Do I have to?
Edna Come and give your Aunty Edna a kiss.
John No.
Edna Come on and give me a kiss, it's not that often that I see you. Come on, that's better, give your Aunty Edna a big kiss. (*She offers her cheek to John*)

John slowly approaches Edna and kisses her wincing as he does so

Edna That's better.
Dot Now go to bed ...
John Yes, Mam. Thanks. Don't hit me, will you?

Edna Rebecca plays the clarinet, did I ever tell you? Is there any more tea, Dorothy?

John exits

Edna freezes

Dot (*mocking*) Is there any more tea?
Doris What's got into you?
Dot Her ... their Edna. She makes me feel right awkward, as if I'm doing everything wrong. As if I'm on show all the time. .... It's like meeting the Queen.
Vic She's all right, she's like us. She started out just like us.
Edna Rebecca speaks German, did I tell you?
Dot But she makes me feel like we're thick or something. Does she think we're thick, Vic? Does she think *I'm* thick?
Vic I don't know what she thinks, do I?
Doris She doesn't like rich food, does she?
Edna I'll get some fresh air.

Edna exits

Dot She thinks we're stupid.
Vic Well, let's be honest, you do talk some rot.
Dot Well, what have I got to talk to her about? And all that stuff about Rebecca. Rebecca this, Rebecca that. The poor kid hasn't got a life, she does everything that your Edna tells her. If he doesn't pass his eleven-plus I'll kill him, I will, I'll kill him. If he ever lets this family down I'll kill him.

Jack enters the scene. It is nineteen-sixty-seven

Doris He failed, Dad.
Jack It's him.
Vic Who?
Jack You. Your side. We've always had brains.
Liz Who has?
Jack We have.
Liz I had the brains, Jack. I had the brains. You had the brawn. You've got the brawn, I've got the brains.
Jack I've got brains, Liz.
Liz But you never use them.
Doris He should go to a special school.
Dot Doris?
Doris Well.
Vic He's not going down t' pit, whatever happens.
Doris They sent Christine Morgan to a special school. She never came back.
Vic So what? I'm not having my lad down a pit, Jack. I wouldn't wish that on a Jap.
Dot Stop shouting at our Doris.
Vic He's going to Secondary Modern and that's that. I'll have a word with him, we'll have a man to man. He can make his career working in a garage.

Jack He should be a prison warden.

Dot Dad?

Jack Prison warden.

Doris Bad company for a young lad, Dad.

Liz When he leaves school, a prison warden.

Jack A good job is that.

Vic Oh yeah, how do you know?

Jack Make a man of him that would. A prison warden.

Dot We've heard you.

Jack He can work wi' me at pit. I've got a shovel waiting for him.

Vic He'll do all right.

Doris You can visit when you want. Mrs Jackson's brother worked in a prison.

Vic I'll see to that.

Liz Vic's too soft with him.

Dot You're too soft with him, and he's having no more comics.

Liz He's been too soft, has Vic.

Vic You buy him the comics. I bought him *Treasure Island* for Christmas and he never read it. He's not interested.

Doris I never liked that.

Liz What's that?

Doris *Treasure Island.*

Liz He'll find his own interests when he gets older.

Dot Does anyone want any more tea?

Doris There's a tart in the kitchen.

Vic Is there?

Doris There's a tart in the kitchen if anybody wants one; if anybody wants a tart, I've brought some, they're in the kitchen. They're lovely, I made them myself. Anybody want one?

There is a pause. Everyone looks at Doris

All No thanks.

Doris They're nice!

The cast freezes

John enters dressed as a twelve-year-old in nineteen-sixty-eight

John (*to the audience*) My Aunty Doris was an awful cook. A year later when I was at Clifton Secondary Modern she made a hundred Bakewell tarts and not one of them got eaten, and she still didn't get the message. I remember nineteen-sixty-eight and the school at Clifton it certainly wasn't modern but it was definitely secondary.

The cast comes out of the freeze

John is very distressed

Dot What's wrong?

John Nothing.

Liz What's wrong?

Dot There is.

Liz What's the matter now?

Doris Does he want a tart, I've brought some?

Vic What's the matter?

John Geek.

Vic What?

John (*beginning to shake and cry*) Geek ...

Vic Now listen, stop it, listen, listen; take a deep breath, calm down and tell me what's the matter.

John Geek Davis keeps picking on me.

Dot (*hard*) Well, pick on him back.

Vic Don't encourage him to fight, Dot, let's bring him up right, shall we?

John I can't.

Dot (*shouting*) Why can't you?

Vic Don't shout at him, he's upset.

Dot I'm not shouting at him, Vic, I'm talking to him.

Doris Look at him, he's all upset, he's a sensitive lad, aren't you? What's he upset for, what's happened?

Dot Who is he, John, who is this Geek Davis?

Liz What sort of a name is that?

John He's a lad.

Vic Is he an older lad?

John Yeah.

Doris I thought as much when he came in; I thought to myself, I bet an older lad's picking on him.

John Everytime ... I ... go out of the house, he comes and gets me.

Doris How long has this been going on?

John Since I went to Clifton.

Liz He should never have gone to that school.

Doris They should send him to a special school.

Liz It's a disgrace, is that school.

Vic And how long has he been picking on you?

John Since the first day.

Vic And have you ever done anything back?

John No.

Dot Right ... I'm going to see his mother. Where do they live?

John I don't know, Mam.

Dot You do. Where do they live, John?

John I don't know.

Vic Why? Why does he hit you?

Liz What has he done to deserve being hit? Nothing. He's done nothing. They're picking on him for nothing.

John He picks on me and he hits me and he shows me up.

Vic Why, what does he do?

John He pulls my ears when I'm in front of the girls and they all call me "Big Ears."

Liz (*kindly, softly*) Oh, that's not nice.

John And they all follow me around calling me "Big Ears."

Doris He should never have had short hair.

Liz Shut up, Doris.

Doris Not with ears like that. He should never have had his hair cut short.

John And he throws things at me, and spits on my coat.

Vic How old is he?

John Fifteen.

Dot Where's he live?

Liz Your grandad'll get him, won't you, Jack?

Jack (*bobbing and weaving, shadow-punching like a boxer*) Jab him, John . . . when you see him, just jab him, no talking, right? Just a jab, and the old one-two. Hit first, ask questions second.

Dot Don't, Dad.

Vic We're trying to bring him up right.

Jack Ar, and he's being picked on. Lad's scared to death.

Liz Do you know them, Jack?

Doris Who is it?

Liz Davis.

Jack I'll find out where they live, and I'll go around there and I'll smash every window in their bloody house.

Liz Your grandad'll see to them.

Jack is furious

Dot I don't want anybody picking on him. He's my son and I love him.

All the family is on tenterhooks

Vic You love him too much; we've got to let him find his own way. Kids are cruel, they say all sorts. (*To John*) Hey kid, listen to this. When I was as old as you, other lads used to call me "Horse Teeth", they did. Because all my teeth had gone bad and I had to have false teeth. That was when I was as old as you.

Dot That's not true, Vic.

Vic It is. An' there was this lad, John, he had a nose that was so big, you know what the other lads used to call him?

John "Big Nose."

Vic No. "Face." They just called him "Face", that's all; and you know what he does now?

John No.

Vic He's an insurance man.

Jack And he gets called a lot worse now than he ever did.

Vic If that's all what's happened we should leave it.

John That's not all.

Dot Why, what else is there?

John I can't tell you.

Vic John, we're your mam and dad, you can tell us anything.

Doris I knew there was something else. Nobody gets that worked up over being called "Big Ears."

Liz He hasn't got big ears, anyway, it's just that his hair is short.

John Today, when I was coming home from football practice with the Robins, he followed me.

Doris Who followed him?

Vic Geek Davis.

John I started to run. There was him, Fig, Jonah and some others who I didn't know, and some girls. I ran across the school field, but Geek caught up and dragged me down, and then they all caught up to us.

Vic And did you try and struggle?

John No.

Dot (*exasperated*) Our John ...

John (*close to tears; it is very hard for him to tell his story*) And then ... and then ... two of them said did I know how to do the "Three-Man-Lift", and I said "No." And then Geek said that this lad could pick up three people at once, and they said that they would show me. And they sat down one at each side, and all these girls came over and Geek said he was going to do the "Three-Man-Lift", and these lads had hold of me at either side and I couldn't move and then they took my trousers down, and all the girls saw me. ... (*He bursts into tears*) Mam ... Mam ... I wasn't doing anything to hurt them. Mam ... Dad?

There is a silence

Vic (*exploding*) Right, that's it! Where does he live? I'm having a word about this. Where does he live? Because I'm not having it, I'm not having that. I want a word about this, I'm not having my lad treated like that.

Jack Burn the lot of 'em.

Dot Look, just leave it.

Vic I'll. ... I'll ... I'll smash every window in their bloody house and that's swearing, Jack, and you'll not often hear me swear.

Liz They should leave him alone.

Vic I will ... I'll swing for that Geek Davis or whatever his real name is.

Doris Davis?

Vic Geek Davis, Doris, are you deaf?

Doris I was just thinking: Davis? I know that name. That must be Bud Davis's son. He went to school with me and our Dot. Oh, the whole family are a bunch of heathens. He's been in and out of prison more times than I've had hot dinners. Ken knows of 'em.

Dot He was a bad 'un was Bud Davis.

Doris I wun't meddle with them, Vic.

Liz Your dad'll have 'em.

Dot My dad's getting past that, Mam.

Doris They once looked after a rabbit while somebody went on holiday, and by the time they'd got back Bud had skinned the rabbit and they'd had it in the pot.

Vic I'm not bothered who they are, they have no right treating our John like that. It's not fair.

Jack is still moving round the room, jabbing senselessly at the air. No-one takes any notice of him

Jack Hey John, remember, one-two, one-two. Jab, see, jab, jab.

Liz He's a good lad; he loves his gran and that's all that matters.

Doris He's got to stick up for himself though, Mam. He can't go through life like a drip.

Liz He's a good lad, I don't want him fighting. I don't want him turning out like your dad.

Jack What's wrong with me?

Liz I don't want him being an animal like you.

Doris Our Dot's too soft with him.

Dot I'm not.

Liz She's too soft with him is our Dorothy.

Vic We want what's best for him, Jack; we don't want him to bring any trouble home but we don't want a drip.

Liz She's too soft with him.

Dot I'm not soft with him. (*To John*) Come here, you, (*to Liz*) I'll show you if I'm too soft with him.

Liz Leave him, leave him, don't hit him.

Dot (*shaking John*) I could hit you!

Rebecca and Edna burst on the stage as if appearing in a musical

Edna We've got some wonderful news, Vic, wonderful. Becky's been accepted at Cambridge. Isn't that fabulous? We're ever so pleased for her, we're taking her to Rome as a treat. Hope everything is fine with you. Come on, Rebecca.

Rebecca Isn't it fantastic news? I'm sure you'll all be delighted.

Edna and Rebecca exit

There is a silence

Dot Go to bed.

John Yes, Mam.

Dot Come here ...

John moves to Dot. She hugs him

Dot I love you kid. I love you. Now go to bed.

Doris starts playing "Happy Birthday" on a kazoo and picks up a briefcase wrapped in birthday paper

The others join in the singing and put on party hats secreted in the table

John Dad, Dad, how does a sailor know there's a man in the moon?

Dot We've heard it.

Vic Our Doris hasn't.

John Aunty Doris, how does a sailor know that there is a man in the moon?

Doris I don't know. Is it because he's a sailor?

Vic What?

John No. It's because he's been to sea.

Jack Useless.

John Been to sea.

Act I

15

Dot He should be on t' telly. He thinks he's funny.

Vic Hey, that's a good joke that is. At least it's clean, not like what he usually comes out with.

John It's because he's been to sea, Grandad.

Jack I'm not thick.

Liz Is he going to open it or what? Can he open it, Doris?

Doris Course he can. Open your present. (*She hands the present to John*)

Dot (*to Doris*) You shouldn't bother. (*To Jack*) Vic's been promoted, Dad.

Doris I like to.

Dot (*to Doris*) You've got no money. (*To Jack*) Still at pit; Method Study.

Doris We've saved up for it.

Dot (*to Doris*) I know but ... (*To Jack*) He loves it. No spade work now, eh?

Jack Watching other men work. I wouldn't have that.

Vic It's good is that, been to sea. Our John's good at jokes. Did you make it up?

John I think so.

Jack Method Study; men don't like 'em.

John starts to tear the paper off the briefcase

Vic That's a great joke that, I'll tell it at work. Make it appear I've thought it up.

Dot You needn't bother.

Jack I wouldn't have a Method Study man telling me what to do.

John finishes unwrapping the briefcase, which looks very expensive

Doris I hope you like it.

John It's great.

Liz It's lovely that, isn't it? It's lovely.

Jack What's he want an handbag for?

Liz It's a briefcase.

Jack I know.

John It's great, Aunty Doris. Thanks, thanks a lot.

Doris Give us a kiss. I'm not your Aunty Edna, I won't bite.

John kisses Doris

Dot (*inspecting the briefcase*) Yes, it's just the job. I don't know if he's got anything worth putting in it, but it's just the job.

Doris It's for his schooling. I saw one in Skegness when we went away. I thought, I'll get our John one of them.

Vic Proper student now, kid?

Doris I was going to knit him another tank top, but then I thought, "No, Doris, a change is as good as a rest."

Liz (*producing a parcel*) And I've bought him a suit.

Doris Smashing.

Liz I saw it in the sale, fifteen pounds. Reduced from ninety-five. It's a bird's-eye pattern.

Dot Try it on for your Aunty Doris.

John Mam?

Dot Try it on.

Liz Leave him. He looks smart in it, Doris. Just right for school.

John I'm not wearing it for school, am I?

Dot Course you are.

John (*to the audience*) I looked like one of the Royal Family in it.

Liz It suits you, you don't want to be like all the others.

John (*to the audience*) I looked like an old man in it.

Doris How's he doing at school?

Vic He's doing all right. We've had his Options meeting to pick his subjects.

Dot He said he wanted to be an actor.

Vic He just came out with it. I didn't know where to put myself.

Jack A bloody actor?

Vic He said he wanted to be an actor or a doctor. So they've got him doing Drama and Chemistry. When we got out of that office I could have gone mad with him. I've spent the last nine months convincing him he isn't going to play football for Leeds.

Liz I want him to be a doctor, then if ever there's anything wrong with me our John'll be able to look after me. I don't like going to t' doctors.

Jack Is he still playing for t'Robins?

Vic He scored four on Sat'day.

Jack Ar.

Dot He's a clown is our John, you have to watch him.

John (*to the audience*) I was with that haircut.

Dot He's a clown, takes after Vic.

Vic I'm educating him, Jack. I give him a new word every time I get the *Reader's Digest*: *Increase Your Word Power*. There's power in words, Jack.

John (*to the family*) My dad's favourite word at the moment is axiomatic.

Doris Oh heck.

Jack I'll trim them hedges if you want, Vic?

Liz Get wrapped up if you're going out.

Vic You can leave it, you know, Jack. I can do it.

Dot Just sit down, Dad, relax.

Liz He looks smart in that suit Doris, he does.

Doris He should get himself a little job.

Vic He's got a paper round.

John I've got myself a job, helping my mother clean up. It's a full-time job. School work is just part-time.

Jack Get a job, then he'll know what work is.

John I know what work is.

Vic Aye, he could watch it all day.

John Anyway, I might leave home and go and live with my gran, eh, Gran?

Dot She doesn't want you. She only wants you because she knows you have to go home.

Liz He can stop when he likes but I'm getting too old now.

John No you're not, you're only twenty-one really.

Liz I wish I was.

Jack She does too much.

Liz Don't start.

John So that's where it comes from. I thought you didn't overdo it?

Liz Well, his grandad's like a cat on hot bricks, he can't keep still.

Jack She should be taking it steady.

Vic She likes to keep active, don't you, Ma?

Liz Well, what am I supposed to do, sit and watch the goldfish all day? I'd end up like our Doris's Ken.

Doris Mother. It's a birthday.

Jack Now, now, you two.

Liz Well, he's such a funny man. We don't ever see your Uncle Ken, John.

Jack Not on a birthday, Liz.

Dot Leave it, Mam.

Liz I mean is he still alive, or is he dead, or has he left her, or what?

Jack When're you getting a new car then, Vic?

Vic Get one next year, Pa, all being well.

Doris is very tender on the subject of Ken; nervously she can't resist rising to the bait

Doris He stays in, he never goes out. We live our own life and we're happy and that's the end of it.

Liz I don't think I've seen him twice since they were married.

Vic Yeah, he's not been out since he lost his teeth in the sea at Torquay.

Doris Don't exaggerate, Mother.

Vic He lost his teeth, isn't that right, Doris? (*To John*) Your Uncle Ken lost his teeth in the sea on the first day of their honeymoon and they didn't speak to each other for the rest of the week.

Doris I don't think it's funny, Vic.

Vic And apparently his suck was worse than his bite.

Dot (*sharply*) Stop it!

Doris It wasn't Torquay, it was Yarmouth. And in any case I've got my dogs; Ken stays in and I look after the dogs. I know he's funny, but we're happy and I don't think there's any reason for Vic to make him a laughing stock. And after I've bought our John that present I don't expect to come here and get humiliated. That cost us thirty-five pounds, that briefcase.

Jack You'll set her off, you know what she's like.

Doris And I don't thank you, Mother, for bringing it up.

Liz (*as if she's played no part*) I've said nothing.

Doris (*close to tears*) I'm not having it.

John Aunty Doris?

Doris I'm going. I'm not stopping here, I'm going. (*She stands, in tears*)

Dot Oh nip, sit down.

Doris I'm not . . . I'm going, it's not fair. I can't make him come out of the house, I can't tell him what to do; do you think I don't want him to come home? It was my dad—my dad said some awful things when we got married.

Liz Your dad never wanted you to marry Ken!

Doris My dad said some awful things and Ken said he'd never forgive him and he hasn't done. And my dad won't take it back and Ken won't take it back.

Jack I'm not taking anything back, he's still a snake as far as I'm concerned.

Dot It was Vic that started all this.

Vic I was only having a laugh, telling the tale.

Doris Well, it wasn't funny.

Liz She's highly strung is our Doris, she always has been.

Dot (*to Liz shouting*) You set her off.

Liz Who are you shouting at?

Doris Well, I'm glad your opinion of Ken's never changed, Dad, because it wouldn't be like you to change your opinion. Me and Ken are happy enough and I'll tell you this, I'll never come up here again as long as I live.

Doris exits in tears

There is a silence

Doris returns, still crying

Doris Forgot me knitting bag.

The others laugh, kindly

Mantovani's "The Way You Look Tonight" softly fades in

John and Doris exit

Liz, Jack, Dot and Vic enter as if returning from the theatre

During the following, they remove their party hats

Liz Oh, wasn't it fantastic?

Vic Lovely, wasn't it?

Liz One of the best nights in years. I'll never forget it, I never will. Come on, Jack, let's dance.

Jack No.

Liz Come on.

Jack I don't want.

Liz Oh, you spoilsport.

Vic Come on, Ma, I'll dance with you.

Dot Look at mi mam.

Vic and Liz dance slowly to the music

Liz Go steady, Vic, you're all over my feet.

Vic Sorry, Ma.

Dot Vic can't do anything right for mi mam.

Liz He's better than your dad, he used to cripple me.

Jack I'm better than Vic at everything.

Dot Where is he?

Liz He's trying on his costume again for me, I thought it was beautiful.

Dot (*calling off*) Come on Errol Flynn, we're all waiting.

Liz I'll have to sit down, Vic, I feel a bit dizzy. I'm not as nippy as I thought I was.

Vic Do you want to dance, Pa?

Jack Get away, you daft sod.

Liz Fantastic. It was a beautiful evening.

Dot Well, I've got to say, I was proud of him. I couldn't see out of my eyes for crying.

John enters. He is dressed as a lion and growling

Vic Look out, "King of the Jungle's" here.

Liz Well, he looks even better close up. He was the best thing in it. There was only one problem: he wasn't on long enough. Why didn't you have a bigger part?

Vic It's his first year in the Youth Theatre, Ma.

Liz Well, you look a million dollars.

Dot (*to Liz slightly anxiously*) Are you all right, Mam?

Liz I'm all right.

Dot You look a bit pale.

Liz It's the weather. I don't like warm weather. I like it when it's cold, put a bit of colour in my cheeks. Eh, John. Eh? Put a bit of colour in your gran's cheeks.

Vic He's French, the playwright, Mam.

Liz (*revelling in the recent memory*) Oh, but he was good.

Vic Yeah, next year they might give him a speaking part.

Jack Ar. He wasn't on long.

Liz He was fantastic, he was the best lion I've seen.

Vic I can remember him at the junior school. He was in *Sleeping Beauty*. He was a tree. He was the only tree that picked his nose.

Dot We know that, you couldn't contain yourself. Every time he came on you started clapping.

Vic Well, I'm proud of him. Hey, can you remember when he was in the Nativity?

Dot Not again, Vic. (*To Liz*) Are you sure you're all right, Mam?

Liz I'm fine.

Vic (*loudly*) "Is there a baby here, the stars are shining so brightly."

Dot Vic, why are you telling me this? I was there.

Vic He shouted that loud you could hear him in the Post Office next door.

Liz He was a good shepherd.

John Did you enjoy it, Grandad?

Jack Well.

Liz It's not your grandad's thing. He's more for sport and horse racing, aren't you?

Jack (*reluctantly*) I didn't like it.

Liz Jack.

Jack Well, I didn't, no use pretending. All that way to Rotherham and he wasn't on two minutes.

John I'll go and take my costume off.

John slowly exits

Dot Dad, be a bit sensitive.
Jack I thought it was a load of rubbish. I couldn't understand it, for a start.
Liz Well, you shouldn't have come, then.
Jack I didn't want to in the first place. That's the trouble with this family;
nobody says what they really think.
Vic Lad's interested in acting, Pa.

Vic exits

Jack It's a woman's job. A nancy's job.
Liz Don't be so crude, Jack.
Jack I'm only saying.
Liz Everybody's not like you, you know; other people have feelings.
Jack It'd be better if more people were like me, you wouldn't put up with
such shit. To be honest, it wasn't my cuppa tea, in fact after our John had
been on I was ready for home. And a lot of others were and all.
Dot Sometimes, Dad . . .

John enters, dressed as a fourteen-year-old. He watches the scene

Jack Always tell the truth, no matter about hurting people. Always tell the
truth. He knows his grandad does.
Dot Yeah, even if it's crippling.

Dot exits

Liz Well, I thought he was fantastic.

Liz exits

Jack Well, I didn't and that's that. He's not bothered anyway, lad's not
bothered. He's gunna face a lot worse than that. (*To John*) He's not
bothered, are you . . . ?

*Jack freezes. John comes forward. The rest of the cast moves into the
background*

John (*to the audience*) My grandad didn't like me being in plays. And when
I started playing rugby he got really confused.

*Rebecca enters. It is early nineteen-seventy-two; Rebecca is a student at
Cambridge and dresses accordingly*

Rebecca Mummy's in the garden with Uncle Vic. Your garden is so small, I
never realized before. You're so close to your neighbours, it's awful; it's
not very private, is it? It's ever so warm out there; it's a sun trap.
John Yeah.
Rebecca Good weather for a study break.
John Yeah.
Rebecca I was going to play Uncle Vic something on the clarinet but you
can't hear for the dogs.
John Might sound a lot better.

Rebecca Uncle Vic is so funny.
John Start a new trend, dog and wind instrument?
Rebecca He's really good at jokes. I'm awful.
John Really?
Rebecca I think your grandfather is teasing the dogs.
John Oh, right.
Rebecca He seems to have a way with dogs.
John He's been surrounded by them all his life.
Rebecca Yes, Uncle Vic is very good at jokes.
John Yeah.
Rebecca Yes. He said he'd like to hear me play. Another time, maybe.
John Yes, he likes Acker Bilk.
Rebecca Really?

There is a silence

What sort of things are you doing at the moment?
John All sorts.
Rebecca I suppose you'll be thinking about jobs soon. Would you like to work at the pit?
John No. I'd like to stay at school.
Rebecca Is there much homework?
John A bit.

There is a silence

Rebecca (*working hard to keep the conversation going*) I sent you a card from Paris; did you get it?
John No.
Rebecca Oh, well, I did send one. We went to Paris, and then we went to Rome. I'd been before but we went with some friends from college.
John Oh.
Rebecca You should see Rome, it's fascinating.
John Is it?
Rebecca I went with Mum before I went down. Almost everywhere you look there are these incredibly old buildings, and monuments, and fountains. It really is fantastic. And the fact that that is the centre, you know, the centre of all this civilization. You'd love it.
John Yeah?
Rebecca You should go.
John Why?
Rebecca Because you'd enjoy it.
John Oh.
Rebecca Have you been to Europe?
John No.

There is a silence

Edna enters

Edna Oh, it's so warm. I think the dogs are sweating. I could certainly smell something out there and I'm sure it wasn't human.

Rebecca I was just telling John about Rome.

Edna Oh, really.

Rebecca He said he hasn't been abroad.

Edna What, not even to Wales?

John No.

Edna What about your mum and dad?

John Not as far as I know.

Edna Really. I thought Vic had been to Scotland during National Service?

John Dunno.

Edna Beautifully clean, isn't it, Rebecca? The house!

There is a slight pause

Rebecca Well you must go, John, because it's unbelievable.

Edna (*answering herself*) Beautifully clean.

John I do most of it.

Rebecca Mother doesn't bother much.

John On my hands and knees.

Edna I wonder if Aunt Dorothy is making any tea, Rebecca? Do you have Rington's, John?

John I don't want to go abroad because I've heard that it smells.

Edna Rome. No. Venice, slightly in summer.

John And the food's not very good. No, we have Typhoo.

Rebecca Where did you hear that?

John I read it in a book.

Rebecca You read it then, you didn't hear it.

Edna Don't believe everything you read, John. Just because something's in a book, doesn't mean that it's entirely true.

Rebecca You should see for yourself. Don't believe others.

John Why should I believe you, then?

Edna Because why should we lie to you?

John Why should anyone lie in a book?

Edna It's not a lie, darling. It's a different opinion. Do you think we could have tea?

Rebecca I think it's amazing. I'd never thought about it before. You're, what are you now?

John Nearly fifteen.

Rebecca And you've never been out of the country.

John I'm not interested.

Rebecca Don't you want to see the world?

John No. I've never been anywhere except Blackpool.

Rebecca Blackpool?

John Yeah, we go there on holiday, and we all sleep in one bed, and we have a potty underneath the bed just in case. Have you ever been?

Rebecca No, actually, I haven't.

John You should go, it's absolutely unbelievable.

Alma Cogan singing "Hernando's Hideaway" plays

Edna and Rebecca exit

The Lights change, coming up on Jack, Doris, Vic, John, Liz and Dot. They are arranged around the table in a tableau that indicates that they are faced with a problem; the scene is reminiscent of pictures of Mafia families. The costumes and lighting are fairly monochromatic, with nothing garish on stage

The music fades

There is silence, broken only by the sounds of a dog barking occasionally off, and the fidgeting of the family

Vic Go on.

John Somebody broke my nose.

Vic Who?

John Dad, why?

Vic Who was it?

John It's not important.

Dot We want to know who it is, we want to know what you were doing for somebody to break your nose.

John Why can't we just leave it and get our dinners?

Liz Because nobody is hungry.

John I am.

Vic We want to know what happened.

John (*sighing*) OK, I was coming back from the cinema——

Dot He's always at the bloody pictures. Him and Tub are always at the pictures.

Vic Let him tell the tale.

Doris What film was it?

John *Zulu.*

Dot It wasn't, so don't lie.

John It was *Zulu.*

Dot It was *Twins of Evil*, because I checked in the paper.

Vic So you shouldn't have been there in the first place.

Dot It was an X certificate.

Doris Disgusting, that.

Dot I'm ashamed of him.

John What have I done wrong? Everyone in the school goes.

Liz I've never liked that school.

Vic And we know about your books.

John (*shocked*) Books?

Vic Books.

John What books?

Vic What books, what books! We weren't born yesterday. Don't give us that. Do I have to spell it out for you?

John (*innocently*) Yeah, I don't know what books you mean.

Vic I mean those books which you keep in the record cabinet. That you'd thought you'd hide from us, that you thought we wouldn't find, those books inside the record sleeves.

John Oh, yeah.

Vic You should have known your mother would find them, she cleans everywhere.

Doris That's disgusting, I think.

John They're not my books, anyway, they're Tub's.

Dot Well, you'd better give them back to him in that case, because I don't want them in this house. In fact I'll tell his mother when I see her and she can come around and collect them.

John I don't think he wants them back.

Dot No, I thought she might not.

John So they can go in the dustbin. I was going to throw them away myself, but I've been busy doing the housework.

Dot Right, Vic, them books—dustbin, I don't want to see them.

John I never looked at them anyway. I'm not interested in that sort of stuff.

Vic Well you've got quite a little collection for somebody who's not interested in them. I counted over twenty.

Dot (*to Vic*) What were you doing with them?

Vic Counting them.

John Well, I hope you've put them all back because they're his dad's.

Vic They're going in the bin and don't try and avoid the issue: get on with the story.

John You brought it up.

Liz Will that chicken be ready, Dot?

Dot It can wait, Mam.

John Anyway I came out of the cinema, and it's been a good night, not brilliant. The film was crap.

Dot clips John

Dot Language at the table.

John Sorry.

Vic Get on with it.

Dot He dramatizes everything.

John So I walk home and these two figures are standing at the top of the hill; I can't see who they are. They stop me and ask me for a chip.

Liz You should keep off chips.

Dot He doesn't have them in this house.

John And the next thing I know there's blood all over my shirt, my nose feels numb and he's hit me.

Vic Who?

John Geek Davis.

Liz (*as angry as her mild manner allows*) Oh, that lad.

Doris The family are a nuisance.

Vic And what did you do?

John What could I do?

Dot You could have hit him back.

John I had a bag full of chips.

Vic That's no excuse.

John What did you want me to do, chip him to death?

Liz You should've stuck up for yourself.

John Gran?

Liz You should.

John I didn't know he was going to hit me. It was pitch black. What do you think he had, a big sign saying "Look out, the end is nigh"?

Jack (*slowly; deadly serious*) It's about time you did something about it, because if you don't, I'm warning you he'll make the rest of your life a misery. While ever our John's around here he'll make his life a misery. Now this is thee grandad telling you. Fight back.

There is a silence

John I don't want to.

Jack (*shocked*) You don't want to?

John No.

Jack (*shouting*) What are you going to do?

Liz Jack, stop shouting.

Jack He'll let everybody in the world shit on him.

Liz Now Jack, that's gone far enough.

John Well, me mam shits on me dad.

Dot Dad, don't get worked up.

Jack Well, it's about time somebody said something about our John because Vic's too lily-livered to do anything about it.

Liz Now don't start.

Vic What do you mean by that?

Liz Jack, you've upset one, don't upset another.

Jack You know what I mean.

Liz He'll lose a friend in Vic if he starts.

Jack Somebody has to say it.

Liz Take no notice of him, Vic, he doesn't mean what he says.

Vic Our lad's been hit, Jack, now I say forget it.

Jack Forget it. He's like a nancy.

John Who is?

Dot Shut up, you.

John I'm not like a nancy.

Liz Shut up.

John Gran?

Doris Dad, stop shouting. We can have a rational conversation. Just stop shouting or you'll make yourself bad.

Vic (*beginning to lose his temper*) I'm warning you, Jack, don't say what you're thinking, because it's not fair. Now I'm warning you. This is my house. I pay the rent here.

Doris You should have bought this house.

Jack You're warning me.

Vic I am.

Jack (*tense*) You're warning me?

Vic I am, yes.

Jack You.

Doris You should have bought this house when we bought ours.

Vic Yes, me.

Jack You're warning me. I've eaten bigger men than you.

Dot Oh, for God's sake, Dad.

Liz Jack.

Dot Dad.

Liz Vic, forget it, forget it. He goes off the deep end and he doesn't know what he's saying.

The atmosphere is tense. Jack and Vic are straining to get at each other, but of course both realize the consequences

Jack I've beaten men like you with double bronchitis. In fact I'll have you now . . . come on, come on here. I'll have you now. (*He gets up*) Come on.

Liz Jack.

Doris You're making my mam bad.

Vic (*standing*) Get out of my house.

Dot Oh.

Vic Get out.

Jack You're warning me?

Vic Get out.

John You're both crackers.

Vic Get out Jack, I'm not having it.

Jack You will have it if you come here. You'll have it on the nose end.

Vic And now I'm telling you.

Jack You're telling me?

Vic I'm not warning you, I'm telling you. Get out of this house and don't ever come back again.

Dot Now stop it, stop it, the pair of you. Stop it.

Liz Vic, he doesn't mean it, do you Jack? Vic, Vic, he doesn't mean it.

Doris Dad, calm down.

Jack I mean it. I bloody well mean it.

Vic Get out!

Jack (*appealing to Liz*) I'm not having him talk to me like that. I didn't have men at the pit talk to me like that. I'm not having some trump Time-and-Motion man talk to me like that.

Vic Why, who are you?

Liz Think of our John. Jack, it's no good him seeing all this, think of the lad. Jack, I'm pleading with you, please, please . . . I'm pleading with you. (*She is extremely upset and begins to cough*)

Doris Dad, just pack it in.

Jack I'm not being shouted at like that.

John Oh no.

Dot (*to John, exploding with rage*) You shut up you, shut up. Otherwise I'll hit you and it won't be like Geek Davis, it'll be a real smack and I'll knock some sense into your head. Watching dirty films, you're pathetic.

Liz Leave him, Dorothy.

John It's like a madhouse.

Vic You've heard your mother, and she's told you to shut up. If you'd got any guts at all we wouldn't be arguing. Why didn't you hit him back, why didn't you run off, are you that thick? For goodness' sake, you're living in a dream world.

Dot All his life is a bloody play.

Vic We must be the laughing stock in the Davis house.

Jack He lives in a Walter Mitty world.

Doris He does.

Dot He's only interested in one thing.

John I'm not.

Dot Making people laugh; well, they're laughing all right. They're laughing right in your face.

John This family? I've got a broken nose and nobody's bothered about that.

Liz What did he hit you for?

Dot He was probably playing the fool. Doing one of those silly walks or whatever he does.

Doris He needs to grow up. He's too highly strung.

John Listen who's talking.

Vic Stop your back-chat, you, my lad.

Jack I've pulled this family up by the boot straps. ... I had nothing, nothing. I've had to fight for every little bit of respect.

Vic (*exasperated*) I don't know what we're going to make of him. Why didn't you have a go back at them?

John Because I'm scared.

Jack Scared?

Doris You're scared?

Dot What are you scared of?

John Being hurt.

Vic (*lost*) I don't know.

John What can I do against Geek Davis? All the kids on the estate are scared of him. He's a right maniac, he's an amateur boxer or something. He just hit me for a laugh. He thinks I'm soft.

Liz You are.

There is a silence

Vic (*lost*) I don't know.

Dot Right. He can stay in this house for a month.

There are winces of approval and nods of satisfaction from the family

John A month?

Dot A month.

John That's my mother's answer to everything, she should have been a judge.

Vic No more dirty books, no more sneaking off to the pictures in a dirty mac. I'll put a stop to that, he can stay in and help me. My car's playing me up, he can help me with that, it's about time he learned to do something technical. I'll show him who's boss in this house. I want to keep my eye on him.

Jack He should take up boxing.

Dot Dad, you've said enough now.

Jack Boxing. One two. Don't ask questions. Bang. (*He throws a short stabbing right*) Bang.

Doris He can help Ken clean his garage out, Vic, if you want him to do some dirty work, as a punishment, you know?

Jack I want to know if we've got a man in the family. I want to know what he's going to do about it? He's farting about in bloody plays.

Dot Dad, please. Honestly. Please. Can we leave it now?

John There's not a lot I can do, is there? I'm being locked up for a month.

Liz He wants one of them things out of the catalogue. They're in our Doris's catalogue.

Doris I don't know what you're on about.

Liz Is it a "Cow-worker"? Get him one of them. How to kick sand in somebody's face in ten seconds a day. (*To Dot*) Don't you feed him?

Dot Course we feed him.

Liz What on, sausage meat?

Dot Mother, we feed him.

Liz He needs fish.

Dot He gets fish.

Liz What sort of fish?

Dot Fish fish.

Liz He needs fresh fish.

Jack He needs milk, meat and fish.

Vic He needs vegetables.

Doris He needs calcium.

Liz He needs chicken and vitamins.

Jack He needs his body building up, he's like a piece of bloody string.

Doris I bet that chicken'll be burnt.

Dot And it's all his silly fault.

John You'd better put another month on my sentence.

Dot Don't be so clever you, you're not too old to get a good hiding.

John I've just had a good hiding.

Liz He needs fish.

Doris I can smell burning.

Dot That bloody chicken.

Music plays

All rush off except John

The music fades

John (*to the audience*) My Aunty Doris was right: the chicken was burnt; so were the spuds, the cabbage, the peas and the gravy. And it was the only Sunday dinner I can remember that consisted solely of Arctic Roll. When my "Bullworker" arrived from the catalogue it was so tightly wrapped and I was so weak that I couldn't get it out of the wrapper. So we sent it back to Kays. But it didn't matter anyway, because my Uncle Ken had some weights in his garage and he said that I could have them. So I started weight training. My dad, in an effort to show off his manhood, got tennis elbow from over-straining with the weights and was off work for three weeks.

The Lights change

It is almost a year later

Vic enters; he is clearly very happy

Vic Ha ha ... I knew it ... I knew it ... I knew he wouldn't let us down. Ha ha ... fantastic. ... Oh, wait till I tell our Edna he's done as well as Rebecca.

Dot enters. She looks at Vic

Dot She's got ten O levels. ...

Vic I'm going to watch *Calendar*, then I'll go and I'm going to phone our Edna. Nine CSE Grade ones.

Dot They're better aren't they?

Vic I knew it, I did, I could feel it in my water. And he said he didn't even try. I knew he would do it. Jarring Jack Jackson.

Dot You're alway over the top, like your Edna. Calm down, your false teeth are slipping.

Vic I'm pleased.

Dot I knew he'd do it.

Vic Yeah?

Dot Of course, it was axiomatic.

Vic (*to John*) Come here, you.

John Don't, Dad.

Vic Let me give you a kiss. (*He kisses John*)

Dot Look at your dad, he'll burst a blood vessel. He's as soft as a brush. He's crying.

Vic Course I'm crying.

Dot You're always over the top. He gets carried away. He's mentally unstable is your dad.

Vic What are you going to do with your qualifications, kid?

John I think I'd like to be a prison warden.

Vic (*to Dot*) Come here, you.

Diane Washington singing "September In The Rain" plays

Vic grabs Dot and they dance. The Lights change—perhaps a mirror-ball effect can be used—to show how transported they are

John, watching his parents dance, is picked out by a spotlight

John (*to the audience*) There was a great celebration in our house the night I got my CSE results. And from then on I could hold my head up on the bus with the lads who went to grammar school. That night my dad had half a lager and my mother had a brandy. They really went to town. And I had my own small celebration. I went out, drank a full bottle of Pernod, kissed Lyn Sutton full on the lips, took her to a disco and returned home at half-one drunk as a skunk. My dad was furious but could understand my feelings. My mother, characteristically, said nothing. She simply hit me in the face with a shoe.

He exits

The Lights change to green, to indicate that we are now in the garden

It is nineteen-seventy-three

Liz, Rebecca, Dot, Jack, Edna and Vic are onstage, sitting in garden chairs. Liz looks very ill and has a blanket tucked round her; Dot and Doris sit looking at her. Jack contemplates the sky. Vic looks warm and contented

There are the faint sounds of birdsong and dogs barking

Dot gets up and tucks the blanket around Liz

Dot Are you warm enough, Mam?
Liz Warm enough? I'm roasting.
Dot (*louder*) Are you warm enough?
Liz Stop fussing.
Doris Is she warm enough?
Dot She's all right now.
Liz You'd think I was a new-born baby with this treatment.
Doris Tuck her in.
Edna That looks better.
Liz Look at me. I'm like an old woman.
Vic You'll be all right, Ma, Dot'll see to you.
Jack I told her she'd overdo it. She's cleaning all the time. She still thinks she's in service.
Liz (*easily*) Shut up, you.
Jack She's made herself bad.
Liz Oh, he's off again.
Jack I'm only telling the truth.
Doris She's warm enough.

John enters; his lip is slightly bruised

John Are you all right, Gran?
Liz I'm smashing, kid. Never felt better. All this fuss over nothing. Your mother. She panics. Have you hurt your lip?
John Messing with them weights.
Vic We're a family of panickers, Ma. I panic at the least little thing.
Liz He's got a bruised lip.
John It's you I'm more bothered about.
Liz (*matter of fact*) I don't know how this family'll go on when there's a bereavement. You've all got faces as long as a wet week and I'm not even dead yet.
Doris Mam?
Liz Well, we'll not be here for ever, will we, Pa?
Jack (*quietly*) Speak for yourself.
Liz He thinks he's Peter Pan, does your dad.

They all laugh uncomfortably

Doris You'll outlive us, you, I don't know what you're talking about.

Edna Don't get a chill, you know, Grandma.

Dot Do you want another sandwich, Edna? There's plenty left.

Doris Go on, get one, help yourself.

Dot There's plenty left.

Vic There's hundreds left. She always makes too many. You'd think she was feeding the whole estate.

Doris There's a tart if she wants one. I've made them with that wholemeal flour.

Edna No thanks.

Doris Rebecca?

Rebecca Yes, I'll have one, they sound nice.

Jack (*quietly*) She's risking her life having one of them tarts.

Doris Oh, somebody wants one of my tarts. (*She moves to the exit*) Put the flag out.

Vic Phone the papers, Doris.

Doris exits

Dot John, you'd better phone for an ambulance.

John (*looking at Liz as if worried about her*) Why?

Dot Rebecca'll need one.

John (*relieved*) It must be Christmas, my mother made a joke.

Liz Our Doris is pleased with herself, isn't she?

Vic She's about to commit an act of genocide, Ma.

John *Reader's Digest* again?

Vic You can't beat it.

John It's unbeatable.

Vic Of course it is.

Dot She's had twins, Mam.

Liz Who, our Doris? I thought they weren't having any.

John }
Vic } (*half-hearing the other conversation; together*)   Eh?
                                                  What?

Dot The dogs have had twins.

Liz Nobody told me.

Dot We did.

Jack She's forgot.

Liz I haven't forgot; nobody told me.

Vic Tina and Trixie.

Jack (*in disbelief*) Our Doris, tut tut tut tut ...

Vic Tina and Trixie?

Liz Lovely names.

Doris returns with a large tray of tarts

Doris Here we are. The feeding of the five thousand.

Liz You didn't tell me, did you?

Doris Tell you what?

Liz About the dogs.

Doris No, I haven't told you.

Liz See.

Doris Our Dot told you.

Liz But I knew you hadn't told me. They think I'm going senile.

Vic We don't.

Doris Here you are Rebecca, take your pick. (*She presents the tarts to Rebecca*)

Rebecca Doesn't anyone else . . . ?

Jack We've had them before.

Rebecca takes a tart and tastes it

Liz . . . think I'm going senile.

Rebecca Actually they're quite nice.

John Wait till they've settled in your stomach . . . you'll not be able to move. They're like concrete.

Doris Hey, you, don't be so cheeky.

Doris exits

John Only joking.

Vic So what's new, Rebecca?

Rebecca (*still chewing*) They're quite nice.

Vic Did you know she's got a first class degree, kid? That's fantastic.

Dot I've brought some wine special, Edna. Blue Nun. Do you like it?

Doris enters

Doris Isn't it warm? Close, isn't it?

Dot Does anybody want any wine?

Liz What, she got a first what?

Edna Not for me Dorothy, really.

John She's passed her exams.

Dot More tea then, anybody? Any more for any more?

Vic Sit down, relax, get some sun on you.

Liz She's as white as a sheet, is our Dot.

Doris Look who's talking.

Edna We think she's going to stay on. She's been offered a research place.

Jack That sun's warm . . .

Edna I think she'll probably stay in Cambridge.

Jack It's a sun trap, this garden. I always said it was.

Rebecca Mum wants to sort all the things out for me, Uncle Vic.

Jack A really nice quiet piece of God's earth this is.

Rebecca She thinks she's living my life for me.

Edna I don't, dear, I only want what's for the best.

Rebecca The best for who, Mother?

Doris How's that tart gone down?

Rebecca Fine.

Doris Do you want another?

Jack She's trying to kill her.

Vic First class honours, that's fantastic, eh, kid?

Rebecca I'm not living my life for my mother, not any more.

Edna (*tensely*) Rebecca ...

Vic Do you still play the clarinet?

Rebecca On and off.

Edna She's very good, Vic, she's Grade Eight. But she's lazy. She needs pushing.

Rebecca I want to travel. I fancy working in India.

Dot India? I've got some place mats made in India. Got pictures of the Taj Mahal on them.

Rebecca Oh really?

Dot They're lovely.

Rebecca I want to see as much of the world as I can. Mummy would rather I was shut away.

Vic University of Life, eh, Rebecca?

Dot (*to John*) Go and get them place mats from India, show Rebecca.

John She dun't want to see 'em.

Vic Are we ever going to hear you play, Rebecca?

Dot Vic, don't, it's not fair.

Rebecca I haven't got my clarinet.

Edna You have dear, it's in the car.

Vic Be nice that, nice bit of music, eh, kid?

Doris She's not going to play, is she?

Vic Be lovely, that.

Edna When she's travelled I think she'll go back to university. She just has to get this wanderlust out of her system.

Liz You never told me you'd had twins, Doris.

Dot I told you.

Liz Just feel me, will you; am I cold?

Doris and Edna dash over to Liz

Doris (*touching Liz*) No, you're smashing, you daft old brush.

Rebecca Is she all right?

Doris She's smashing.

Rebecca I'm never going back, Mum, you go back if you're so keen. I'm up to here with it. (*She pauses*) I'll go to the car.

Rebecca exits

Edna So what about John? What's next after A levels?

Vic He's just been in another play, Edna: *Dark of the Moon.*

Liz I want him to be a doctor.

Edna Has he thought about teaching, Vic? Has he ever thought about being a teacher? Very few people make it in creative professions, you know, Vic? It's something to fall back on. ...

Dot Just at the moment, Edna, he's into this weight-lifting lark. But it won't last, it never does, and you can't keep him away from the cinema.

Edna Rebecca had no interest in the cinema.

Doris She's not going to play sommat classical is she?

Edna That sun is so hot.

Dot Vic, go and get that sun hat from Blackpool for your Edna. It says "Kiss Me Quick" on it, Edna. You'll be all right with that.

Edna I think I'll just stand in the shade. (*She moves to stand in the shade*)

Jack Beautiful garden.

Dot If ever I'm feeling a bit low, I sit at the window and I look out into my garden.

Vic That's when she's finished cleaning up.

Dot Shut up, Horse Teeth.

Vic Come here, give us a cuddle.

Dot What for?

Vic Because I hate you, what do you think?

Liz (*jokingly*) Oh Vic, steady on.

Vic Do you want a cuddle as well, Ma?

Vic cuddles Dot, simply and not sloppily; they are clearly in love

Jack (*to John*) Still playing rugby?

John Ar.

Jack Still doing plays?

John Ar.

Jack How's weights going?

John Allrate.

There is a silence

Jack Let's have a feel at your arms.

John No, get away.

Liz Come here, I'll have a feel. (*She feels John's arms, then moves a hand to his head and ruffles his hair*) Oh yeah, lovely, that is.

John Don't say it, Dad.

Vic Like knots in cotton.

Dot He can't help himself.

Vic sings half a verse of "You Make Me Feel So Young" to Dot

Liz Can he whistle? Because he can't sing.

John You tell him, Gran.

Vic I know, Ma, *Over the Hills and Far Away.*

Liz Yes. That's where I want you to sing it. (*She begins to chuckle at her own joke and continues to laugh throughout the rest of the scene*)

Doris Look at my mam. She's having a little titter to herself.

Dot Yeah, at Vic's expense.

Liz He thinks he's such a good singer.

Jack (*musing*) Do you know, that sun is lovely.

Dot Vic's as soft as a brush.

Liz He'll never be one of us though will he? He'll never be a member of this family, no matter how hard he tries.

Vic (*laughing, slightly hurt*) This is my family, Ma. This is my family.

Liz This is my family, Vic. This is my family and I love them all ...

Dot (*warmly and kindly*) Look at my mam, she's as pleased as punch.

Liz (*musing*) Over the hills and far away ... (*She begins to laugh*)

The rest of the family join in the laughter; it should be the gentlest laugh possible

> *Rebecca enters upstage with her clarinet; she plays Gershwin's "Summertime" very movingly*

The Lights fade

There is the sound of birdsong

Curtain

ACT II

Alma Cogan singing "Why Do Fools Fall in Love?" plays

The cast enter and take up positions around the stage in a dim light

It is now nineteen-seventy-five

Dot is C, sweeping dust into a dustpan. She is agitated. Vic is upstage, watching Dot. Liz sits in a chair upstage. Although the audience can see and hear her, she is, in fact, dead. The rest of the cast watch Dot

John wanders downstage, much more casually than before; he, too, watches Dot

The music fades. The Lights come up on the scene. There is a silence

Dot I don't believe it!

Vic Look at you, you're killing yourself.

Dot After all we've done for him? I'm behind with my routine today.

Vic You don't have to do that every day.

Dot I've got all upstairs to do yet. There's no tea on; he's really upset me, he has.

Vic Why, what's he done?

Dot He knows I have a good tidy around on a Wednesday.

Vic You do the same every day.

Dot I'm finished at one on Tuesdays.

Vic (*in disbelief*) You do the *same* every day.

Dot He has to come and upset me on a Wednesday?

Vic It wouldn't matter which day he came; you do the same every day.

Dot (*ignoring Vic*) Sundays are usually my big day for washing.

Vic You wash every day. You can see through my trousers because you wash them every day. You're washing away all our clothes.

Dot There's no tea on.

Vic I heard you the first time.

Dot (*flustered*) So I don't know what you're going to have.

Vic I'll have nothing.

Dot You can't have nothing.

Vic I'm not hungry.

Dot You must be hungry.

Vic How do you know if I'm hungry?

Dot So you're not hungry?

Vic I'm starving but I want to know what's been going on.

Dot stops cleaning

Dot (*to John*) Tell your Dad.

John You're the one making a song and a dance about it—you tell him.

Dot Tell him!

John No.

Dot Tell him.

John No.

Dot He's been kicked out.

John That's not true.

Dot He's been kicked out because he's pathetic, and we'll be the laughing stock . . . I can just see your Edna's face. I can just see her smug expression when she finds out. . . .

John Mother, no-one will be a laughing stock, because it's not true. So, hard luck, you're wrong again, you're wrong, you're wrong, you're wrong.

Vic Is it true?

John No.

Dot (*in a rage*) Tell him, tell your dad, because I'm disgusted with you, I am. I wash my hands of you. In fact I'll tell you something: I haven't got time for you. I'm finished with you. I don't care what you do. He knows what things are like with my nerves since my mam died. I'm finished with him, I am. Finished.

Liz watches the action with interest

John Great, well, thanks for your support. I'll not bother coming home again, it'll save all the hassle.

Dot It'll suit me.

John Will it?

Dot It will.

John You couldn't stop crying when I left.

Dot I won't cry when you leave this time.

Liz tuts audibly

John Won't you?

Dot No I won't. You can go now for me.

John You'd have a stroke if I did.

Dot I wouldn't.

John You want to know my every move.

Dot I don't.

John Don't you? You could have fooled me.

Vic (*exhausted*) Will somebody please talk to me?

John It's my mother.

Liz She's always been the same.

John She's crackers.

Liz She takes after her dad.

John (*moving to Vic; controlled*) It's no big deal, my mother's getting carried away as usual, because she only half listens to what anybody has to say. ... Unless you're talking about lace curtains or nylon sheets or double glazing my mother's not interested. ... She ought to be on *Tomorrow's World* as an expert on dust. (*To Dot*) Why d'you clean up all the time?

Dot Do you think I like it? Do you think I want to? You'll come a cropper, you will.

John Will I?

Dot Yes.

John I won't.

Dot He's throwing opportunities away. I could have gone to grammar school, you know, but we didn't have any money to pay for me. What is there in my bloody life? All I do is stay in this rotten house and clean up. What have I got in my life?

Vic I think I'll go out and come in again. It's like a madhouse. I thought all the shouting and bawling was a thing of the past. (*He walks about the stage, unable to bear the emotional tension*)

Dot He's been thrown out of college. He's been there a year, he's done no work. I could hit him.

John That'd be helpful, wouldn't it?

Dot Don't think I won't smack you, my lad.

John Play something different, will you?

Dot (*becoming calmer*) And shall I tell you why he's been kicked out?

John Here we go, more lies.

Vic Let's listen.

Dot Because he can't keep away from the women.

There is a silence

John looks slightly embarrassed

   Now?

There is another silence

   He can't control himself, that's the problem. He's always after the women.

Vic (*carefully*) Well don't look at me as if it's my fault.

Dot He can't control himself.

Vic That's not my fault.

Dot When he's away from home he thinks he's Errol Flynn.

John I don't.

Liz (*to herself*) I love Errol Flynn.

Dot He's done no work all year and we're living on tinned ham.

Liz (*to herself*) I love Errol Flynn ...

Dot Living on tinned ham? If anybody knew.

Vic We're not *just* living on tinned ham.

Dot As soon as he gets with that lot he's in that college bar, drinking, messing about, making a fool of himself. I'll tell you this, we haven't sacrificed all we have for you to be sleeping with every girl you speak to.

John Where's all this come from?

Dot I knew as soon as I saw him.

John What?

Dot As soon as he came through that door I knew something had changed.

John OK, so you're psychic.

Liz (*to John*) He wants to watch what he's doing.

Dot I'm your mother; I know you better than you know yourself.

John You should have gone to college for me, then.

Vic What he does in his own time is none of our business.

Dot We don't know what he does.

John I don't do anything.

Dot We don't know what he does.

John Why has this come up?

Dot You've been too soft with him, Vic.

Liz (*to Vic*) He always has been.

Dot He's failed everything.

John I haven't.

Dot We had that phone put in and he never rings. He should have gone down the pit like the rest of the family instead of thinking he was sommat special. All our family's worked at pit, on both sides. He's bloody disgrace, and he smells.

Vic (*to John*) Have you?

John What?

Liz They should have hit him more often.

Dot He has.

Vic (*shouting*) Will you listen for a minute?

Liz (*to no-one*) Always shouting in that house.

Dot It's him.

Liz He should have been a prison warden.

John OK, I failed my foundation course and Philosophy and that's about it.

Vic Right.

John And I failed the Sociology course.

Vic Right.

John And Education, Psychology and Maths.

Vic And what about Drama?

John I did all right, I got a C-minus.

Vic (*sarcastically*) Oh, congratulations, you must be over the moon.

John All I have to do, and I've been trying to explain this to my mother, is submit a piece of work and they'll accept me back. I've written a play and it can be used as part of the course work. I've been upset about my gran an' all, you know, I couldn't work; all I could do was my play.

Vic Right, now we know. (*He calms down*) We've all been upset. Now, what's it about, this here play?

There is a pause

John It's about a night club.

Vic About bloody ... who's gunna be interested in that? And that's going to get you back to be a teacher, is it? You're bloody barmy, you're living in cloud cuckoo land. You listen to me: stop living life in the fast lane.

John Teacher training college is hardly the fast lane.

Vic I don't want any lip.

John I didn't go to drama school because of you.

Vic It's sommat to fall back on, we all agreed on that, now you know we did.

Dot He's disco mad.

John I like to watch.

Dot He's one of them perverts.

Vic Can we just ... hang on ... can we leave it? Now I've had a day of it at work and all. So why don't we all help your mother get finished cleaning up, and then we'll have some tea.

Dot It's only tinned ham.

Vic (*sarcastically*) I love tinned ham.

John (*to the audience*) My dad could eat anything, he had bionic teeth. He needn't have bothered taking the ham out of the tin, he could bite straight through it.

Vic (*histrionically*) I loved tinned ham.

Vic exits

Dot exits

The Lights change

John turns to address the audience

John (*to the audience*) It was nineteen-seventy-five and a lot of things had changed. For a start I'd got a brace of A levels and a place at teacher's training college. And my mother was right, I'd lost my virginity. In fact I lost my virginity as many times as I could. (*He pauses*) College was great because nobody died and the future as a teacher of Drama looked bright and secure. And as my Aunt Edna had said, "It was something to fall back on." Back at my home my grandad had moved in with us. Gran had died.

Liz gets up. Only John can see her

Liz (*after a pause, to John*) I went in for a hysterectomy, but it was too much. It was a nice quiet funeral. But the weather was awful. A small family affair, with a small reception at our Dorothy's. I was surprised Ken actually made it. But I suppose he had to; our Doris was in such a state she couldn't walk. I warned 'em. When you love like we did ... (*she returns to her seat to watch the action*)

Vic, Jack and Dot enter. Jack is carrying a pair of garden shears

Doris enters to them

Doris I've put some flowers on my mam's, Dot. I've been down to the ... you know? I've put some new flowers on. We can take turns, putting them on.

Dot Are you all right, Dad? Are you going to sit down for a minute and have a sandwich?

Jack I'm all right. These shears need seeing to.

Dot You look a bit flushed.

Jack I'm right.

Doris Come and sit down, Dad.

Jack I don't like to sit. My mind thinks on it when I sit; I like to keep moving.

Doris He doesn't like going to the ... you know?

Vic You'll tire yourself out.

Jack (*close to tears*) It's just that ...

Dot We know, Dad, we know ...

Doris Don't ...

Jack When I see the garden, when I see the sun on the garden, I think ... I can't help it.

Vic Hey, come on.

Jack completely breaks down, crying the cry of a man who has never cried and does not want to

The rest of the family is on the verge of breaking down too

Jack I'm sorry ... I'm sorry ... Oh God, Dot, I wish she was back ... I do.

Dot I know.

Jack I wish she was back ...

Doris Don't, Dad.

Jack Oh ... why didn't He take me?

Dot Come on ...

Liz Then I'd've been left on my own?

The family sits Jack down and comforts him

Jack She must have been in such pain. For years—and she never told anyone.

Dot I know, I know.

Jack Why didn't He take me?

Liz He was always selfish.

Jack Oh, I miss her.

Doris He's setting me off.

Jack I can't help it.

Dot I miss her too.

Jack I miss her.

They all start to cry, or are near to tears

Liz My family?

John Don't cry, Grandad.

Dot Oh, Mother. (*She hugs John, crying*) Oh Mam, my mam, I miss her, John, I miss her.

John (*comforting Dot*) I know, Mam, I know.

Jack (*attempting to compose himself*) Do you know what's the worse thing? I never told her I loved her. She never knew.

Vic I miss her.

There is a silence

Liz I never thought I'd hear Vic say that.
Dot She knew.
Jack No.
Dot She did.
Jack I never told her.
Vic She knew, Pa, you didn't have to tell her.
Jack I did. But I was too bloody bull-headed.
Doris She knew.
Liz I knew, Jack.
Jack If she was here now I'd tell her. . . .
Dot No, you wouldn't, you'd be out in the garden pottering about or watching the racing, and that's what she'd expect you to do. My mam was like me; she didn't go in for all that lovey-dovey stuff.
Liz It would have been nice once in a while.
Doris Eh, come on, Dad, she wouldn't want you to be ruining your life, would she?
Dot No, she wouldn't, she wouldn't've wanted that. . . .
Doris No, she wouldn't.
Dot Get some fresh air. I'll get his coat.

Dot exits

Doris Why don't you take him a walk, Vic?

Jack, recovering, wipes his tears away with a white handkerchief, watched by the others

Vic Do you want to go a walk, Pa?

They all freeze, holding the moment

The Lights change

John breaks out of the freeze

John (*to the audience*) And they walked around the block, and played cards, and talked, and drank tea, and cut the lawn, and listened to records and drank more tea, and dunked ginger biscuits. But the pain was too deep. It was rooted, you could almost see it. You could touch it with your fingers. It had a hold of my grandad and was pulling him down, forcing him nearer to the ground, twisting him like the stump of an old tree. And they walked and drank tea and listened to records, and I wondered how many hands of pontoon you have to play to erase sixty years of love. I thought the pain would be over in a blink, but I was wrong—it was with us forever.

John returns to his place in the frozen scene

The Lights change

It is now a few months later

Dot enters, full of energy. She addresses the whole family

Dot Do you know what I've been thinking?

Vic What do you think we are, mind readers?

Dot Don't you think it would be nice if we all went away together this summer?

John (*frightened*) Eh?

Dot All of us.

John The whole family?

Dot I think we should go away.

Vic We could visit our Edna in Gloucester.

John And slash our wrists.

Doris Go away where?

Dot Well, we can't take my dad to Blackpool, so I thought we'd have a change.

Liz He loves Blackpool; take him to Blackpool.

Doris A change?

Dot I thought it would be really good if we all went in a caravan.

John (*horrified*) Eh?

Dot All the family together like old times. We could get a six-berth at Feathers in Whitley Bay.

John Me as well?

Dot All of us.

Liz Good idea. You need a break. Get you out of that house.

Jack Well, I don't know.

Doris (*loudly, as if Jack is deaf*) It'll be a change, Dad. A change.

John I'm not going.

Dot Why not?

John I don't want to.

Dot Can't you just do it for us?

John Oh yes, it sounds wonderful, doesn't it?

Doris It'll be cosy.

John Like living in a lift.

Liz (*to herself*) I've always liked Geordies.

John Yes, but can you imagine it?

Vic I think your grandad would like it, kid.

John Tough.

Jack (*slowly*) He doesn't have to come for me.

John See.

Dot He's coming.

John I'm not.

Liz Lovely people they are, Geordies.

Doris I think it'll be good.

John A week in a caravan?

Doris Yes. Sounds exciting; I like caravanning.

John I'd rather be buried alive.

Vic It could be arranged.

John My dad's a funny man, give him a round of applause.

Dot Stop it, you. Who do you think you are?

John I'm me, who're you?

Vic Oh, we're off?

John Yeah, we are.

Doris What's wrong with him?

Liz He's on drugs.

Dot He's crackers.

John Listen who's talking. I don't wash the curtains fifteen times a day. Why don't we become nudists? It would help my mother's arthritis.

Jack (*cautiously, as if sensing a row brewing*) I think I'll have a walk.

Dot It's raining, Dad.

Jack I think I'll have a little stroll.

John What, another?

Vic Just stop it.

Liz He wants belting when he's like that.

Jack He should have had more belts, he should.

John That's your answer to everything, isn't it? If it moves, hit it.

Doris Come on, kid. Uncle Ken might come.

Jack If he's going, I'm not.

Doris Come on, the whole family. Your gran'd like it.

John My gran's dead.

Liz tuts audibly

Dot He's selfish.

John Me?

Dot You.

Vic I think we've heard enough.

John *Selfish.* Hang on! You took no interest in my school work. All you said was "Get it done." You didn't even let me do my homework at the dinner table, you said it was too messy. I revised for my A levels in the loo.

Vic Why do you exaggerate everything-bloody-thing?

Dot He's changed.

John How very observant.

Vic Let it drop.

Liz I think it would be nice, a few days by the sea.

Dot He's changed, and it's not for the better.

Jack (*as if lost*) I'll get some fresh air.

Doris It's throwing it down.

Jack I'll cut your hedges.

Vic It's raining, Pa.

Jack It'll not take long.

Vic Pa?

John There's no hedges left, he cuts them every day.

Jack I'll just trim 'em.

John The grass is taller than the privets.

Dot I never thought I'd see a son of mine wearing mascara.

John I wondered how long it would be before that came up.

Dot Mascara!

John I only wore it for a laugh.

Doris What's he been wearing mascara for?

John A laugh.

Vic He's crackers.

Jack I don't want to be in a caravan with him if he's wearing make-up.

John I'm not; my mother's got the wrong end of the stick ... again.

Liz He should never have gone away.

Dot And I'll tell you something else while I'm at it. Don't think we don't know when you're lying to us.

John OK, I admit it. I'm a member of the KGB.

Dot He lies, he does, Doris.

Doris (*philosophically*) Everybody does.

Dot "Don't come and see me at college, Mother, I'm busy"; "Don't come that week I'm doing something"; "No, I can't come home, I'm rehearsing"... I was surprised you made it to the funeral.

Liz She goes too far.

John Look, you reap what you sow. You pushed me, you wanted me to go away, and, all right, maybe I've changed, but so what? And what makes you think that being a close family and not changing is so wonderful? Look at yourselves: what makes you think you're all so perfect that there's no room for change?

Vic Well, if wearing make-up is a change for the better you can stick it.

John Look at this house.

Liz It's a lovely house.

John You're never out of it. You wear it like a coffin. It's suffocating you.

Dot That's why we want to go away.

John Into a caravan or a boarding house? It's the same thing ... it's *worse*!

Liz I always wanted to stay at the *Metropole*.

John (*to Jack*) And look at him.

Liz But we never did.

John Jack the lad. How long is he going to sit and mope about my gran? (*To Jack*) Hey, you, let's have a box, now, shall we, just me and you; you'd be wheezing like an old fart.

Vic John?

John (*to Jack*) Did you think she'd never die? Because you're acting like you never expected it to happen. She's been dead nearly a year.

Liz (*to John*) Nine months ... I've been dead nine months, don't exaggerate.

Doris Nine months.

Liz Thank you.

Dot (*to John*) Can you hear what you're saying?

John For nine months he's been walking about as though dead lice were dropping off him. I thought he was supposed to be a hard nut?

Vic Don't be bloody pathetic.

John Hey, Dad, don't get carried away; your false teeth might drop out.

Vic Stop it.

John Might give us all a nasty bite.

Doris All this over a holiday?

Vic I won't forget you for that.

Dot It's been coming this has, Doris, it's been coming for ages.

John My dad's got the most frightening false teeth in Europe.

Vic I won't forget you for that.

John I've heard you.

Dot He knows this family's still upset but he's not bothered about anybody but himself. He knows what the situation's like with my dad living here and he's not bothered.

John Why is he here? Why doesn't he go back to his own house?

Doris He doesn't like it there on his own.

Liz (*easily*) Too many memories.

Dot He's not bothered.

John No, I'm not. You're right, for once. In fact, do you want to know something?

Vic Here we go.

John I wish you were *all* dead. All of you——

Dot We will be if you keep on. He's driving me to my grave.

John —because we'll never be free until we're born from test tubes. And maybe one day you'll understand what I'm on about.

Doris You've got your whole life ahead of you; one week in a caravan isn't going to hurt.

Vic I don't understand him.

John I don't want to spend one day in a caravan. Not with you, nor my dad, or the Queen, the Pope or anybody. I couldn't think of anything more horrible than a week in Whitley Bay. And while I'm on my hobby-horse let me tell you for the millionth time that I don't like cheese and egg when it's cooked in the oven, or fry-up, or bacon and tomato dip or tinned bloody ham. All right, Mother? Do you understand? The world is a big place, it's even bigger than this house.

Liz I always fancied Greece.

John And if you lot want to go and sit in a box on Tyneside watching the rain, and playing happy families, and listening to my mother go on and on about the price increases in Marks and Spencer's and how she can't get her curtains to hang straight, then go, go now. And if you fancy walking with him (*he indicates Jack*) to St Mary's lighthouse and back a million times a day talking about what my gran would have thought about it, good for you. But I'm not. I refuse my consent and, no matter what you say, nothing, and I mean nothing, will change my mind.

Dot Don't come then.

Liz He's changed, he has. I liked him better when he was younger . . . He was always a nice little lad; he was the apple of his gran's eye.

Doris Well.

Doris stands, saying nothing, then exits

Vic Now we know.

Jack I think I'll get a blow of fresh air.

Dot It's still raining, Dad.

Jack Shall I make us all a cuppa tea?
Vic (*shouting*) Just sit down, Jack. (*Calmly*) Let's sort this one out.
Dot (*to John, pleadingly*) Will you come?
John No.
Dot Please, kid, please.
John No. I'll never go on holiday with you again, ever.

The Lights change; we are on the beach at Whitley Bay. It is evening

The sounds of a high wind and stormy sea can be heard

   All exit except Jack, Liz and John

Liz hands Jack a coat, which he puts on. John puts on a windjammer

Jack is stoic and silent

John Not a bad caravan, is it? Cramped but cosy.

Jack is silent; his face shows his reactions to John's speech, though his mind is with Liz

   Came down here yesterday. Nice, i'n't it? After we played snap and that. I came down for a read. Heavy stuff; Camus, *A Happy Death*.

Jack is still silent

   Not many laughs. (*To the audience*) No man ever used silence like my grandad, he made Pinter seem loquacious.

There is a silence

   (*To Jack*) All that sea?

Jack does not respond

   A boat there, look.

Again, Jack does not respond

   I use them weights, you know? I've got them in my room at college.

There is a silence

Jack I was never right by her. I never did anything right. (*Pause*) I was never any good around the house. (*Pause*) She bought a wardrobe. And we couldn't get it upstairs. So I sawed the banister rail off. She went mad.
Liz (*enjoying the memory*) I can remember.
Jack (*after a pause*) Look after your mother if anything happens. (*He pauses*) There's a blank space on the head stone. It's like an open bible. Liz's name is on one side, the other's a blank, just waiting for me.

There is a silence. Jack and John hardly look at one another

   Don't ever forget where you came from.
John No.

There is another silence

Jack I never knew my mother.
John No.
Jack I didn't belong anywhere.
John No.
Jack She calmed me down.
John Yes.
Jack I had a job as a grocer's lad when I first saw her. (*His voice softens*) Never forget where you come from.
John I don't feel like I belong at college. Everybody seems really clever. Makes me feel stupid.
Jack Ar?
John And I don't belong at home any more.
Jack (*as if his mind is drifting*) No.
John We had this discussion the other week about whether a rational man should ever hit anybody. This tutor got me so wound up, I could have hit him.
Jack Tha should have.
John (*after a pause*) I'm sorry about what I said back home. It was pathetic.
Jack Ar.
John Is it true, didn't you have a family?
Jack I had a step-father. One day he took a belt to me in the street. I never forgot that. When I was twenty-one, I took him into the street and gave him a hiding. Don't ever trust anybody. And if people think bad of you give them good reason to think it. You've done well. I never expected thee to go as far as you have, it's sommat I don't understand. Thee just remember two generations ago this family had nothing.
John Sounds like a Dickens novel.
Jack I'm serious.

There is another long silence

Jack He's still around, that Davis.
John I'm not interested.
Jack Married now.
John Good for him.
Jack Eric Allport's daughter. He was up in court last month.
John (*as if uninterested*) Oh ... ?
Jack It was in the paper. Gone into somebody's house where his ex-wife was staying with her new fancy man and broke his nose.
John I think the wind's getting up.
Jack Hit 'em while they're taking their coats off. One-two. ... The whole family are scum.
John Well, we can't all be brain surgeons.
Jack Scum.
John They're probably all right you know, really.
Jack They're a bad lot. He had a baby to Lyn Sutton. Then he left her.
John Well, that's all behind me now.

Jack A quick one-two. And it's over.
John Live and let live.
Liz You'd better go back, Jack.

There is a silence

Don't want you catching a chill.

There is a silence

Best get back and then our Dot'll make you some supper.
Jack I miss her.

The Lights change, bathing the stage in blue

The sound of the wind gets louder

John, Liz and Jack are "blown" off the stage

Dot, Edna, Vic and Rebecca are "blown" on to the stage

The wind noise fades

The Lights come up on the house once more. The family is having tea. Dot stands near the doorway, as if she is about to exit into the kitchen. She appears to be agitated

Dot Does anybody want Branston Pickle?
Vic We love it up there, Edna.
Rebecca In a caravan?
Vic We love caravanning.
Dot Does anyone want any corned beef?
Rebecca Isn't it overpowering, Uncle Vic?
Edna I don't think I'd like a caravan holiday.
Vic That's what our John thought.
Edna No. It would be too claustrophobic for me.
Rebecca Mother doesn't like to be hemmed in.
Dot Spring onions, anybody?
Vic We love it.
Dot Does anyone want any luncheon meat? I've got some.
Vic (*to Dot*) I'll have a piece of that blackberry pie afterwards.
Dot You won't. The pieces stick in his teeth, Edna.
John (*to the audience*) I'd just finished my final year's Teaching Practice when Burke and Hare dropped in on us for a surprise visit.
Dot Are you sure you've had enough, Edna?
Edna Absolutely.
Dot Would you like another piece of ham? It's lean. I got it from Denis Richards. His mother's blind. The butcher. Nice man, isn't he, Vic?
Edna No, thank you, Dorothy.
Dot Are you sure? You've hardly eaten anything. Nice man. Eh, Vic?
Vic His mother's blind, Edna. She's eighty-five.

Dot Rebecca, go on, have a bite.
John (*to the family*) She still hasn't got over that tart.
Vic And that was five years ago.
Dot Go on, it'll not kill you.
Rebecca No, I'm fine.
Edna Rebecca doesn't eat meat.
Dot Oh, is she ill?
Rebecca No, I——
Dot (*to John*) We like to eat, don't we, kid?
John Yeah, even when we're not hungry.
Dot I'll save this up for tomorrow then, our John can have it in a fry-up.
John (*to the audience*) Fry-up?
Dot I love it when he's at home, Edna, college holidays, I love it.

Dot exits

Vic So what's new in the world, Rebecca? Not shooting off to India again, are we?
Rebecca Not any more, Uncle Vic. I'm working as a nursery nurse and Mike and I are very happy.
John What does Mike do?
Rebecca He's a doctor. Mercury research. I'm not sure of the detail. Atmosphere pollution, that sort of thing.
Edna Rebecca is her own person, Vic; she had a career ahead of her and she's just let it go.
Vic Well, if it's what she wants.
Rebecca I had to let it go. I wasn't good enough, so I stopped. I've explained this to my mother a thousand times.
Vic Are we likely to see a wedding in the family soon?
Rebecca That's a touchy subject, Uncle Vic.
Edna I don't like them living together.
Vic Well, that's what they do nowadays. I wish me and Dot had had a trial period. It would have saved all this heartache over the last twenty years.
Rebecca You don't mean that.
John He does.
Vic I do. (*He crouches on the floor to eat*)

Dot enters

Dot Don't sit like that, Vic, you'll get indigestion. Sit up properly when you eat.
Rebecca My mother's one of the two remaining eminent Victorians.
John My mother's the other.
Edna (*ignoring the bait*) I would have some more tea, Dorothy. It's lovely tea.
Dot It's Early Grey, our John likes it.
John I'm trying to educate them.
Vic (*sarcastically*) He thinks we need it.
Edna It really is lovely tea, I don't think I've ever had it before.
Rebecca You have, Mum.

Edna Have I?

Rebecca Mike and I have it.

John I went to Benidorm on an "Eighteen-to-Thirty" holiday last summer.

Rebecca Oh, how awful.

Edna Did you have to go? Was it part of the course or something?

John No. I went because it was cheap.

Vic He flew out and then went around Europe.

Dot He's completely insane, our John, Edna, didn't you know?

John It was great.

Dot I don't mind Early Grey.

Rebecca Oh, I couldn't.

John No, you might meet a working class person and we couldn't have that.

Rebecca What do you think I was doing in India? The people there had nothing.

John There are people here with nothing.

Vic (*easily*) Yes, us, we've got nothing, Rebecca. We're living on tinned ham at the moment.

Dot Sit up, Vic.

Edna No, I don't like Spain: too sticky.

Dot We've never been.

Vic We've been to Eastbourne.

Dot I like Eastbourne.

John I went up to Madrid, have you been?

Rebecca No.

John Saw *Guernica* at the Prado, have you seen it?

Rebecca No.

Dot I like Eastbourne ... and Whitley Bay.

John It's massive.

Dot Eastbourne's not too big. But it's a long drive.

John Then I went to Toledo and I hitched across Europe.

Edna I don't like Spain.

John Did you see the Dali exhibition?

Rebecca No.

Vic sips his tea and makes a noise

Dot Don't make a noise when you drink your tea, Vic, it's rude.

Vic I'm not.

Dot You are.

John Is there any biscuits?

Dot Have you ever been to Eastbourne?

Edna No.

Dot We like it, don't we, Vic?

Vic Eastbourne?

Dot We like it.

Edna Never been.

Dot Sit up, Vic.

John I didn't know that Kokoschka and Hitler applied for the same course at art school, did you, Rebecca?

Rebecca (*surprised*) No.

Dot He makes a noise with his false teeth, don't you, Vic? I think his gums must have shrunk, and when he drinks he makes a noise. It sounds like his teeth are rattling around in his head.

Edna I see.

Dot Awful in public.

Vic Our John's trying to make us more cultured, Rebecca.

Rebecca Good. Educating you, is he? You should travel, Uncle Vic.

Dot I don't like what he likes, I think it's rubbish.

Vic It's different.

Dot I'm getting awful pains in my chest, Edna.

Vic He treated us to the theatre for my birthday.

Dot It was awful.

Vic It was at the *Grand*. Terry Griffiths. *The Comedians*. I thought it was fantastic.

Rebecca Did you see the Jasper Johns exhibition?

John Yeah, I thought it was crap.

Rebecca Really?

John I didn't see it.

Dot I like Donald O'Connor.

John My mother likes the musicals.

Dot I don't like what he likes.

John Trevor, Dad.

Vic Trevor Griffiths, that's it.

John So you're co-habiting, Rebecca?

Rebecca At the moment.

Edna (*changing the subject*) You've got a wonderful garden still, Dorothy.

Dot My dad sees to it.

Edna How is he?

Dot He's moved in permanently now. The house was too much for him.

Rebecca Have you sold the house?

Vic It was council, Rebecca.

Rebecca Really?

Vic Yeah, it was a council house.

John That means you have to pay rent.

Dot We don't see much of him. He comes in for his dinner, then goes a walk, then he comes back for his tea. Then he goes and sits at the bottom of the street. He counts the cars. Then he comes in and reads a cowboy book.

Vic He doesn't like to be a nuisance.

Dot He isn't.

Vic No I'm not saying he is.

Rebecca So what's next for John?

John I'm going to the moon.

Rebecca You've really changed in the last few years.

John Do you think so?

Rebecca Don't you think so, Mum?

Edna Well, he's certainly got bigger.

Vic He's written some plays, Rebecca, did you know?

Edna I hope they have a story.

Rebecca Mum hates *Godot*.

Vic He's sent one to Yorkshire telly.

John I haven't heard owt.

Edna I used to like the theatre, but I don't go now. Plays today are so depressing.

Rebecca It's quite amazing—the difference.

Dot We don't know who he is half the time. He's crackers.

Vic He's doing an extra year.

Dot I don't know where he gets his brains from.

Vic He gets them from my side of the family, Rebecca.

Rebecca (*to John*) Yes you've changed.

Doris and Jack enter. They have obviously been walking vigorously. Jack looks flushed but not ill; Doris is lively and cheerful

Jack Ar ... that's better. Bit of fresh air.

Doris Just been for a walk.

John (*to Rebecca*) Did you think I'd always be eleven?

Rebecca Not exactly.

Doris It's ever so close outside.

Jack A walk, lovely. Take the dogs, stretch their legs.

Doris It's muggy, close. We've had a nice stroll, haven't we? Down to the ... you know.

Dot How are the flowers?

Doris They look lovely, don't they? Looks really nice.

Jack and Doris sit down; Liz watches them

John (*to Rebecca*) Whenever you come here you make mi mam 'n' dad feel inferior, did you know that?

Vic John?

John It's true.

Vic Take no notice of him, Rebecca.

Rebecca Well, if I did, I never intended to.

John Well, that's how it is. The best china always comes out when you're here.

Doris It's special, isn't it?

Edna (*changing the subject*) How's Grandad?

Jack Tired.

Edna I was just saying that the garden is as lovely as ever.

Jack What?

Vic The garden——

Edna It's as lovely as ever.

Jack Nice little piece of God's earth.

Dot I was on about Eastbourne.

Doris I don't like it.

Vic I knew she'd say that.

Dot She doesn't like it.

Edna I was saying: I've never been.
Doris No.
Edna No.
Doris No ... I don't like it. Too quiet.
Dot She likes a bit of life.
Doris I like a bit of life.

Doris exits to the garden

John It must be me; I over-compensate.
Rebecca What for?
John My dismal failures.
Rebecca I've never thought of you like that.
Vic He's a slow starter.
John Look out for the joke.
Vic It's not a joke, he's a slow starter. Like I am.
John He means late developer.
Rebecca You were just different to us, that's all. I never saw it in any other way.
John We had nothing in common.

Doris enters

Doris It's muggy, you know what I mean? Muggy. Your clothes stick to you. Muggy.
Dot I don't like it when it's muggy.
John Now I've got nothing in common with my mam and dad.
Vic He has.
John I haven't.
Jack Is there any corned beef?
Dot Do you want some?
Jack I'll have some. After.
Vic Dot's dad's always doing that. He asks for something, she gets up, then he says, "I'll have some after."
Dot Do you want any corned beef, nip?
Doris I don't like it. Gives me heartburn. I want a rest. My dad's walked me to death.
Edna Has he?
Jack I haven't.
Doris He has ...
Dot Don't let him overdo it.
Edna Be careful you know, be careful.
Vic He's as fit as a fiddle, aren't you, Pa?
Jack (*easily*) I'm not.
Vic He's as fit as a fiddle.
Dot You shouldn't let him overdo it, Doris.
Jack I'm as fit as a fiddle.
John We eat off the floor when you're not here, we don't even have plates.
Dot He's crackers.
Vic It's clean enough.

Dot Oh, he's off again.

John My mother's doing a university degree, Rebecca, did you know? In cleaning up.

Vic She's a BC: Bachelor of Cleaning.

Dot I need a VC living with you lot.

John I'm off for a shit.

John exits

Dogs can be heard barking in the distance

Doris Very close. And the litter, have you seen it? (*To Dot*) Hear, can you hear?

Dot What is it?

Doris The dogs are barking; they need a drink.

Vic I can't hear anything.

Dot Our Doris can hear 'em. She knows them dogs.

Doris They're barking, they want something.

Jack (*getting up*) Have they had a drink? I'll do it.

Dot Have a minute, Dad, they're our Doris's dogs.

Vic Sit down, Pa.

Doris They need a drink.

Doris exits

Jack I'll do it. She can't be doing it all.

Vic Sit.

Dot They're her dogs.

Vic Rover, stay.

Dot They're a nuisance, them dogs.

Vic Dot? Don't.

Dot (*becoming anxious*) Our Doris thinks more about them dogs than she does about people. She talks to them.

Vic Oh, she's off: "My nerves are bad."

Dot She makes me sick, she does. Always on about them dogs.

Vic Her nerves are bad, Edna.

Edna How are your hands, Dorothy?

Vic They're bad, Edna, she can't keep her hands out of water.

Dot (*showing Edna her hands*) Look. Arthritis. And my nerves.

Vic She'll get that all through her body.

Dot My mother had it, all through her body.

Edna Your mother had cancer as well, though, didn't she?

Dot I sometimes wonder.

Vic She worries herself.

Dot I think about it . . . awful pains in my back. Awful. And my nerves . . . shocking, Edna.

Vic She worries herself sick about it. I've told her to see a specialist.

Edna I know . . . You should see someone.

Vic We're dropping to bits, Rebecca.

Rebecca Young at heart, though, Uncle Vic.

Vic That's us, young at heart. But you've got to be, Rebecca. Look at me, I'm crawling about all day on my hands and knees following a machine; you've got to be young inside.

Rebecca At least you'll always have a job, Uncle Vic. Count your blessings. We're not sure how long Mike's research post will last.

Vic That's the only good thing about it. There'll allus be coal around here.

Doris enters

Doris They've had a drink, that's what they wanted, they wanted a drink. I heard all that barking and I thought, "I wonder what they want?" I thought my dad had given them a drink, and he thought I had, and neither of us had. Anyway . . .

Vic They've had one now.

Dot They've got a dog next door, Edna. All day long, yap yap yap.

Edna I don't think I could stand it.

Vic A collie, a border collie.

Edna I like the quiet.

Doris You get used to it.

Dot Yap yap, gets on my nerves.

Vic Dot's nerves are bad.

Dot Yap yap . . . I don't know why our Doris brings 'em up.

Doris My dad likes to walk 'em. That's why I bring 'em.

Dot She brings 'em with her, they mess on the lawn.

Doris I only bring 'em for my dad, our Dorothy.

Dot I don't mind barking, but I can't stand the yapping.

Doris You've no need to worry, I won't bring them again.

Dot It'll suit me.

Doris I'll not bother coming if you want.

Vic Take no notice, Doris, she's all wound up.

Dot She won't, Edna. You can't talk to our Doris.

Dot exits

Doris And what if I end up like my mother?

Doris exits

Edna Better to be on the safe side.

Vic (*shouting*) Dogs do bark!

Rebecca (*to Edna*) You have had Earl Grey.

Edna I don't remember.

Rebecca You had it when you visited Mike and I in Newbury.

Rebecca exits

Edna I did not!

Edna exits

Vic (*shouting*) Dogs do bark!

Jack Vic's right.

Jack exits

Vic That's the first time you've agreed with me, Jack, in twenty-five years.

Vic exits

There is a silence

John and Liz enter. John is wearing his graduation suit, as at the beginning of the play. Liz begins dusting the furniture used when the family were having tea, and returning the items to their original positions, if necessary

Liz I never liked it when they came to visit. I always liked to keep out of the way. And that tea service, did you see that? I bought that. It was a wedding present. (*She pauses*) I bet you didn't know that I'd paid for my own funeral.

John I never really thought.

Liz Of course you didn't, you were too busy floating about in a world of your own. You never really bothered about us, not since you went to comprehensive school.

John That's not true.

Liz Self, self, self.

John I wanted to do well.

Liz I'd have been proud of you if you'd been a vagrant.

John Well, why didn't somebody say something?

Liz It's your dad, always pushing.

John It wasn't his fault.

There is a silence

Liz Did your mother get my records?

John She plays them all the time.

Liz I had nearly five hundred of them in my loft. I'd saved them up over the years, seventy-eights they were. I used to play them to you. Draw the curtains on a Sunday afternoon, and have an ice cream.

John "But don't tell your mother."

Liz That was it. And we'd listen to the records. Kay Starr, Alma Cogan.

John (*remembering*) Kay Starr, *Bonaparte's Retreat*.

Liz Uncle Ken bought me that, it was his favourite ... (*She pauses thoughtfully*) Your mother said I spoilt you.

John You did.

Liz Well, that's what grandparents are supposed to do.

John (*surprised*) Is it?

Liz He always wanted a son.

John Is that why?

Liz (*as if her mind is drifting*) Always wanted a son.

John We've always been nearer to your side of the family, haven't we?

Liz Vic's mother died when he was very young.

John I didn't know that.

Liz His dad married again; she had children of her own. I don't think they were fair on Vic.

John You never liked my dad, did you?
Liz Vic was all right. Too wishy-washy for me. He wants everybody to like him. And they would if he didn't try so hard.

There is a silence

John I couldn't get back, you know, at the end? I was at college. I couldn't get away.
Liz You could have.
John I had my finals.
Liz He was all right.
John Was he?
Liz Tough to the last.
John Yeah.
Liz He never made a fuss. Never once made a fuss. Did you?

> *Jack enters. He has his hair slicked back and almost looks younger than he did when we last saw him. He, too, is dead, but moves about the stage quite normally. He kisses Liz on the cheek*

Jack No.
Liz (*as if her mind is drifting*) Never once made a fuss.
Jack No.
Liz He did everything he wanted to. (*To Jack*) Didn't you?
Jack Ar.
Liz He did what he wanted.
Jack Ar.
Liz And he didn't let anybody pick on him.
Jack No.
Liz No regrets.
Jack I left eight hundred pounds.
Liz Well, you couldn't bring it with you.
Jack Eight hundred.
Liz Was everything else paid for? All the arrangements?
Jack Ar.
Liz Good. I didn't want our two to have unnecessary trouble.
Jack I saved it up for a rainy day.
Liz It'll come in handy. They could split it. Our Dot could get some new curtains.
Jack They looked after me. Our Dot bathed me, dressed me, fed me and tucked me up in bed. They looked after me, they did.
Liz They're two grand lasses.
Jack They are.

There is a silence

Liz You know what I regret, Jack?
Jack What's that, Liz?
Liz I never went abroad, not in all my life. I never went abroad.

John (*to the audience*) My mother and Aunty Doris were gutted when my grandad died, and it was the first time I'd seen my dad cry. Jack had a violent stroke—it didn't surprise me, everything he did was violent—and after months of my mam and Doris nursing him, and me trying to massage life into his now sparrow-like legs, he passed away. Fifty-two years of pit work had finally killed him. I stayed on an extra year and magically turned a lowly Teaching Certificate into a Degree. It was nineteen-seventy-eight, and I remember seeing Geek Davis. He was married now; they had two kids and he was as round as a beach ball. As we passed in the street Geek nodded and said, "Hello". I said nothing. I turned, grabbed him by the throat and hit him full in the face; he fell to the floor like a sack of shit ... and as he looked up at me, his wife screaming and babies shouting, I kicked him full in the chest.

Jack Yes, give him what for!

Liz What are you playing at, you're supposed to be educated!

John (*to the audience*) I know. For two months after I felt so pathetic that I didn't go out of the house.

The Lights change. It is now nineteen-seventy-eight

Vic enters, wearing a smart suit. He is close to tears

Vic Oh ... fantastic, wasn't it? Ha, ha, I knew you'd do it. Jarring Jack Jackson.

Liz He's on about that film again.

Jack What film?

Liz *That's My Boy*: Jerry Lewis.

Jack I never liked him, he's like a nancy.

Liz He was always going on about that film.

Vic (*to John*) When I saw you up there with them others, oh, I was proud.

John You were the only one who clapped.

Vic I was proudish.

John That's not a word, Dad.

Vic It is.

John No, it's not.

Vic It is, proudish.

John (*anxiously*) It isn't a proper word, Dad.

Vic It is ... it is ...

John All right, it is then.

Vic Proudish is a word. Somewhat proud. I looked it up. Proudish.

John Where, *Reader's Digest*?

Vic Dictionary.

John Why did you stand up and clap?

Vic I just did.

John I know, I saw you. Two thousand people and you are the only one to give a standing ovation. It's embarrassing.

Vic Don't start today.

John It was bloody embarrassing. And my mother. What was she playing at? I wish you'd never come.

Vic It was our day.

John I wish I'd never gone.

Vic Your mother was crying. Doris was crying. I was crying. I'd never seen anything like it, all that pomp and circumstance.

John It's a load of old rubbish.

Vic I said to your mother, when I'd sat down, "I think we'll go away. I think we'll go abroad."

Liz Always fancied Greece, I did.

Vic Spain. That's what she said. She said she'd always wanted to go to Torremolinos.

John Go to Paris.

Vic Can't speak it.

John You can't speak Spanish.

Vic No, but they speak English; the French don't like us.

John Learn French.

Vic Me? No, I'm too old.

John Go to night school. Do something, Dad, you're not stupid, you're bright. Don't wallow in it. Do sommat different. Re-train, you're young enough. Run a night class for jokes.

Vic *Comedians.*

John Unquestionably.

Vic No, I knew when they merged areas there'd be redundancies. And there's millions of tons of coal to dig. They don't need me. Besides I use all my mental skills keeping up with your mother.

Liz She should never have had them dogs. They killed you. You tired yourself out with them dogs.

Jack They're good dogs.

Liz They make her house stink.

John I'll buy you a tape; you can learn French.

Liz She lets them sleep at the bottom of the bed.

Vic No, I'm not learning any other language.

John (*nastily*) Well, waste away then.

Vic (*warningly*) Not today, please not today. Let's just have one day without any arguments.

Liz They had separate beds; what sort of a marriage was that?

Vic When we pulled up at the university my heart was beating. All those old buildings, all that brain power. I felt really small, you know. Really small. And then that car pulls up at the side of mine. A Rolls, wasn't it?

John A Bentley.

Vic And I could see them look down their noses at us. They looked at us and they thought, "Oh, look at that, they've only got an Hillman Minx." And then when it came to it she only had a pass degree; I looked down the booklet and she only had a pass.

John They're nice people, Dad.

Vic And she's looking at us like they think they're it, and she only had a pass. I could see 'em looking at my cheap suit and thinking.

Liz I could have done with separate beds with you.

Jack Ar.

Liz You did nothing but kick. You'd twitch and then kick me; I used to kick you back.

Vic A second-hand Hillman'll do for me.

Jack I was asleep, didn't know I was doing it.

Liz Kick, kick.

Liz and Jack exit

John Where's my Mam?

Vic She's sweeping down the path. She's got a job working for the council.

John Funny.

Vic He was a doctor, him in the Bentley. He had "Doctor on Call" in his windscreen. And I've worked at the pit all that time, dreaming of sommat happening for you. That's why I stood up and clapped.

Dot and Doris enter. Both are smartly dressed; Dot is wearing John's academic gown and cap over her own clothes. They are behaving very girlishly

Dot That's about it, that should do it.

Vic That's why I stood up and clapped.

Dot (*referring to the cap and gown*) I think the whole street should have seen it; I've swept all the way down to Rattigans.

John Oh, no.

Dot I feel very good in it. I might get one.

Vic Have you been sweeping up in that?

Dot Course I have.

John You're an embarrassment.

Dot No, I'm not.

Doris We're only having a laugh. I've had it on. I felt really intelligent, didn't I, nip?

Dot She's had it on.

Doris I have. I thought, I'm having a go with that, see if any brains rub off.

Dot She's been running around the garden in it.

Vic I bet she looked like a bloody witch.

Doris I came out with a long word. Mississippi. Didn't I, nip?

Dot That's a long word.

Vic Elastic, that's a long word.

John Please?

Vic It stretches.

John You're all embarrassing.

Dot Don't be so touchy.

John Well you are. Jesus Christ.

Dot We're just family having fun. And stop swearing.

Doris Don't spoil it.

Vic (*angrily*) He always does.

John (*to Dot*) She's embarrassing.

Dot She?

Liz enters

Liz She's the cat's mother. (*She sits*)

Doris She's the cat's mother is what my Mam'd say.

John I don't believe you lot. Just tell me this: is there a history of mental ill-health in this family? I'll keep an eye out for the symptoms. I mean my grandad's dad might have been a madman.

Doris Don't be so sensitive.

John It's her, my mother. She's round the bend. She tells everybody our business.

Dot I don't.

John She told that woman in the office my life history and we only went to ask her where to park.

Dot I didn't.

Vic He'll spoil it.

John You'll have to learn to keep your mouth shut when I'm with other people, Mother.

Dot Why?

John Because they don't want to hear you come out with a load of old bloody rubbish. I was talking to the Head of the Education faculty about something and my mother came up to me and asked me if I'd had a shave.

Dot Had you?

John Don't be funny, Mother. It dun't suit yer.

Dot Well, it didn't look like you had to me.

John The poor bloke didn't know where to look.

Vic Well, if he couldn't deal with that he shouldn't be in education.

John Dad, that's not the point.

Dot All right, then, know-all, what else have I done?

Liz She'll never let go of him.

John The whole day was awful.

Doris I thought it was lovely.

John I wanted to die. My mother asked the Bursar's wife if her two-piece was from Marks and Spencer's.

Dot I was making conversation.

Doris It was a lovely two-piece she had on.

Dot It wasn't from Marks. She said it was, but it wasn't.

Vic She's a Marksist, your mother, John.

John I should have left home and never come back.

Doris He should have had a shave.

John I'll tell you this, I'm never coming home again. I can't stand it.

Dot Did you see her hair?

Doris Awful, wasn't it?

Vic (*to John*) It was your idea for your mother to put the gown on. You were the one who was embarrassing. You thought it was funny.

John I wasn't the one who was shouting "He's doing an MA" at the top of my voice, was I?

Doris I heard that.

Vic She's proud.

Dot I got talking to this woman and then some others came out onto the grass and they were talking loud. And she was all snooty.

hter had got a

many hadn't

"

a shame, but

ot to pay.
me eight
We'd all
is taking
nd I can
ere. I'm
on. The
ingness,

r mam
ink we

never
elf a
ting.

o to

y,

64

There is another silence. Eve

Dot I'll make some tea, sha
Doris Oh, lovely. I'm dying
    cup when we were there
    spread, Vic?
Vic It was, Doris. It was,
Dot Do you want a drink
John (*lightly*) I don't kno
    I'll have a cuppa Earl

There is a silence

Dot I'll make some tea a
Vic I could eat a horse -
Doris I'm a bit peckish -
John I am a bit, yeah. I
Liz He should be allow
Vic I stood up and clap
    clapped.
Doris We could have a
    a game of Scrabble?
Liz He stood up and
Jack He's as soft as a
Dot I wish your Edna
Vic She sent a card -
Dot I wish they . . . w
    course she is)
John I'll play Scrabb
Doris I don't cheat -
John Not much. Y
    last one? It was a
Vic Clapter.
John That's it, clap
Doris It's a word -
John She means a
Doris Clapter, like
John I'm not play

There is a pause

Doris (*softly*) I d
Dot Our Doris i
Liz She's all rig
Vic Bloody clap
Doris (*rememb*

There is anothe

Dot Can you r
Vic I can.

Doris Which one was she, nip?

Dot Her in that C and A print.

Doris I thought that was awful. Didn't suit her.

Dot She just came up to me and told me that her daughter had got a teaching job in Bath.

Vic I saw her, she came and told me.

John She told everybody.

Doris Reminded me of your Edna.

Vic *She* was embarrassing.

John Yes, but she wasn't *my* mother.

Dot And she kept going on about this teaching job and how many hadn't got jobs, and she says, "Has he got a job?" So I says, "No."

Vic Playing her along?

Dot Like you do. . . . No, I says he hasn't got a job. "Oh that's a shame, but it's hard". And then I said, "He's going to do an MA."

Doris I heard that.

Dot But she didn't hear, so I shouted it to her.

Vic Her face dropped a foot. Everybody looked over.

Doris You could have stood on her lower lip.

John But she shouldn't have told them!

Vic Why?

John Because I'm embarrassed because I can pay. Because I've got to pay. . . . My grandad slogged his bloody soul-case out and left me eight hundred pounds. Three others from our college had applied. We'd all been offered places. None of us had got a grant. And that money is taking me out of here and I'm not like you. You've pushed me away and I can never come back. (*He indicates his head*) I've left you, up here. I'm Rebecca now, that's what I am; I'm a Martian. And it just goes on. The gap getting bigger and bigger and bigger, until there's just nothingness, silence. And I love you, Christ I love you, but it does me in.

Dot Stop that.

John (*exasperated*) Oh Jesus.

Vic We've always known that you'd go. You have to go. Me and your mam have always known that you wouldn't stay here. What did you think we wanted for you?

John I don't know, Dad.

Vic Whatever we did we did for you. We never did you any harm.

John Not much. I didn't know what sex was until I was nineteen. Whenever the subject came up here, mi mam coughed and you made yourself a coffee. No wonder we're all "fucked up", and don't worry, I'm quoting. It's safe, I'm quoting.

Vic Mis-quoting. I read books and all. (*He pauses*) You don't have to go to college, kid, to read books.

John Where are we going as a family, Dad? Where are we going?

There is a silence

Vic I don't know; I just don't understand you. You had to spoil today, didn't you?

There is another silence. Everyone looks uncomfortable

Dot I'll make some tea, shall I?

Doris Oh, lovely. I'm dying for a cuppa. I thought we'd be able to have a cup when we were there but the spread was very poor. Wasn't it a poor spread, Vic?

Vic It was, Doris. It was, yes.

Dot Do you want a drink, kid. Earl Grey?

John (*lightly*) I don't know why I bother trying to explain. . . . Yes, yes . . . I'll have a cuppa Earl Grey.

There is a silence

Dot I'll make some tea and then we'll have a bit of a bite.

Vic I could eat a horse.

Doris I'm a bit peckish. Are you, kid, are you peckish?

John I am a bit, yeah. I'm peckish.

Liz He should be allowed to do what he wants with his life.

Vic I stood up and clapped. I must be going around the bend. Stood up and clapped.

Doris We could have a game after tea. We could play Scrabble. Who wants a game of Scrabble?

Liz He stood up and clapped.

Jack He's as soft as a brush.

Dot I wish your Edna could have come.

Vic She sent a card. It's a nice card.

Dot I wish they . . . well, you know . . . I'm not upsetting myself . . . (*But of course she is*)

John I'll play Scrabble on condition that you don't cheat, Aunty Doris.

Doris I don't cheat.

John Not much. You're like my dad—you make words up. What was the last one? It was a classic.

Vic Clapter.

John That's it, clapter.

Doris It's a word. Clapter. It's what an audience does at the end of a play.

John She means applause.

Doris Clapter, like laughter. "There was a lot of clapter."

John I'm not playing with her, she cheats.

There is a pause

Doris (*softly*) I don't.

Dot Our Doris is crackers.

Liz She's all right, she is.

Vic Bloody clapter?

Doris (*remembering*) Oh, I don't know. We've had some laughs.

There is another pause

Dot Can you remember when she sat in the garden?

Vic I can.

Dot It was that summer your Edna was here. Can you remember? Rebecca had just got a first and Vic was going on about it. I knew then he'd get a first . . . I knew it.

Doris I can remember. (*She sits on the arm of the sofa*)

Vic The good old days, eh, Doris?

Dot I knew he'd get a first.

John I didn't get a first though, Mam, I got a two-one.

Dot I'll put the kettle on.

Vic (*easily*) It'll not fit you.

Dot takes off the gown and hands it to Doris. John sits on the sofa

Dot Here, you'd better have this or I'll be cleaning up in it.

John That's another thing, isn't it? I was the only one in my group who bought his cap and gown.

Vic Well, we didn't know you could hire 'em.

Doris It's a once in a lifetime thing, isn't it?

Vic Course it is.

Doris Here, I'll have it if you don't want it; I can make some curtains.

Dot (*becoming very emotional*) I wish, you know . . .

Vic (*comfortingly*) Don't set yourself off.

The Lights change

Dot, Doris and Vic freeze

John moves from the sofa to an armchair. He addresses the audience

John That was the last time I spent summer at home. We sat in the garden and everyone took turns in trying on my cap and gown. It was also the last time I saw my gran and grandad so clearly in my head; I don't hear them as often now, and as time has gone by I've almost forgotten what they looked like. I'm not even certain of how much I've told you is the truth. Our memory plays such tricks. But I did get an MA and the only teaching job I could get was at the comprehensive down the road. So I start teaching Drama on Monday.

The Lights change

John sits in the armchair

The rest of the cast comes out of the freeze. Dot is very upset

Dot They would have been proud.

Doris Yeah.

Dot Anyway.

Liz Is she putting that kettle on or what?

Liz exits

There is a silence

Vic Anyway.

Dot I can just see my mother's face; she would have been having a little titter to herself.

Doris Yeah, she would.
Dot (*crying*) I miss 'em ...

Doris stands and comforts her sister

I miss 'em ...
Doris Yeah ...

There is a silence

Vic (*breaking the sombre mood deliberately*) So what is there to eat, buggerlugs? I'm starving.
Dot (*steeling herself emotionally*) Why, what do you fancy, Horse Teeth?
Vic I just fancy getting me teeth into a slice of tinned ham.
Dot (*happily*) Oh ... you little devil ...

Frank Sinatra singing "You Make Me Feel So Young" plays

Dot, Doris and Vic exit, leaving the cap and gown draped over the sofa

John is left alone, sitting in the armchair

The Lights slowly fade to black

CURTAIN

FURNITURE AND PROPERTY LIST

ACT I

On stage: Sofa
Dining table with drawers. *In it:* party hats
Dining chairs
Armchairs

Off stage: Vacuum cleaner **(Dot)**
Polishing cloth **(Dot)**
Garden clippers **(Jack)**
Duster **(Liz)**
Knitting **(Doris)**
Cup of tea **(Edna)**
Clarinet **(Rebecca)**
Teacups
Saucers
Plates
Cutlery
Kazoo **(Doris)**
Briefcase wrapped in birthday paper **(Doris)**
Party hats **(All)**
Parcel **(Liz)**
Garden chairs **(Stage Management)**
Blanket **(Liz)**
Large tray of tarts **(Doris)**

ACT II

On stage: As ACT I

Off stage: Dustpan and brush **(Dot)**
Garden shears **(Jack)**
Duster **(Liz)**
Jack's coat **(Liz)**
Windjammer **(John)**
Teacups
Saucers
Plates
Cutlery

Personal: **Jack:** white handkerchief

LIGHTING PLOT

Practical fittings required: nil

Various suggested interiors and exteriors in the same basic setting

ACT I

To open: General interior lighting

Cue 1	**Lyn Sutton** exits *Lights fade, then come up on tea scene*	(Page 6)
Cue 2	**Edna** and **Rebecca** exit *Lights change*	(Page 23)
Cue 3	**John:** ". . . off work for three weeks." *Lights change*	(Page 29)
Cue 4	**Vic:** "Come here, you." *Mirror-ball effect; spotlight on John*	(Page 29)
Cue 5	**John:** "She simply hit me in the face with a shoe." *Lights change to green*	(Page 30)
Cue 6	**Rebecca** plays *Summertime* *Fade lights*	(Page 35)

ACT II

To open: Dim light

Cue 7	Music fades *Bring lights up on scene*	(Page 36)
Cue 8	**Vic** and **Dot** exit *Lights change*	(Page 40)
Cue 9	**Vic:** "Do you want to go a walk, Pa?" *Lights change*	(Page 42)
Cue 10	**John** returns to the frozen scene *Lights change*	(Page 42)
Cue 11	**John:** "I'll never go on holiday with you again, ever." *Lights change*	(Page 47)
Cue 12	**Jack:** "I miss her." *Bring up blue light*	(Page 49)
Cue 13	The noise of the wind fades *Bring up lights on indoor setting*	(Page 49)

Cue 14	**John:** "... I didn't go out of the house." *Lights change*	(Page 59)
Cue 15	**Vic:** "Don't set yourself off." *Lights change*	(Page 65)
Cue 16	**John:** "So I start teaching Drama on Monday." *Lights change*	(Page 65)
Cue 17	**John** is left alone *Lights slowly fade to black*	(Page 66)

EFFECTS PLOT

ACT I

Cue 1   As ACT I begins   (Page 1)
Music from the late 1960's plays. Fade when ready

Cue 2   **Dot** exits   (Page 6)
"Hernando's Hideaway" plays

Cue 3   All laugh   (Page 18)
Fade in "The Way You Look Tonight"

Cue 4   **John:** "You should go, it's absolutely unbelievable."   (Page 23)
"Hernando's Hideaway" plays

Cue 5   When ready   (Page 23)
Fade music, bring up sound of dogs barking

Cue 6   **Dot:** "That bloody chicken."   (Page 28)
Music plays. Fade when ready

Cue 7   **Vic:** "Come here, you."   (Page 29)
"September In The Rain" plays

Cue 8   **Vic** looks warm and contented   (Page 30)
Faint sounds of birdsong and dogs barking

Cue 9   As the Lights fade
Birdsong   (Page 35)

ACT II

Cue 10   As ACT II begins   (Page 36)
"Why Do Fools Fall In Love" plays. Fade when ready

Cue 11   **John:** "I'll never go on holiday with you again, ever."   (Page 47)
Sounds of high wind and stormy sea

Cue 12   **Jack:** "I miss her."   (Page 49)
The sound of the wind gets louder

Cue 13   **Dot, Edna, Vic** and **Rebecca** are "blown" on to the stage   (Page 49)
Fade wind noise

Cue 14   **John** exits   (Page 55)
Sound of dogs barking in the distance

Cue 15   **Vic** exits   (Page 57)
Fade dog noises

Cue 16   **Dot:** "Oh ... you little devil ..."   (Page 66)
"You Make Me Feel So Young" plays

MADE AND PRINTED IN GREAT BRITAIN BY
LATIMER TREND & COMPANY LTD PLYMOUTH

MADE IN ENGLAND